Cambridge Elements

Elements in the Philosophy of Georg Wilhelm Friedrich Hegel
edited by
Sebastian Stein
Heidelberg University
Joshua Wretzel
Pennsylvania State University

HEGEL AND COLONIALISM

Daniel James
Technische Universität Dresden

Franz Knappik
University of Bergen

Shaftesbury Road, Cambridge CB2 8EA, United Kingdom

One Liberty Plaza, 20th Floor, New York, NY 10006, USA

477 Williamstown Road, Port Melbourne, VIC 3207, Australia

314–321, 3rd Floor, Plot 3, Splendor Forum, Jasola District Centre, New Delhi – 110025, India

103 Penang Road, #05–06/07, Visioncrest Commercial, Singapore 238467

Cambridge University Press is part of Cambridge University Press & Assessment, a department of the University of Cambridge.

We share the University's mission to contribute to society through the pursuit of education, learning and research at the highest international levels of excellence.

www.cambridge.org
Information on this title: www.cambridge.org/9781009587181
DOI: 10.1017/9781009587143

© Daniel James and Franz Knappik 2025

This publication is in copyright. Subject to statutory exception and to the provisions of relevant collective licensing agreements, with the exception of the Creative Commons version the link for which is provided below, no reproduction of any part may take place without the written permission of Cambridge University Press & Assessment.

An online version of this work is published at doi.org/10.1017/9781009587143 under a Creative Commons Open Access license CC-BY-NC 4.0 which permits re-use, distribution and reproduction in any medium for non-commercial purposes providing appropriate credit to the original work is given and any changes made are indicated. To view a copy of this license visit https://creativecommons.org/licenses/by-nc/4.0

When citing this work, please include a reference to the DOI 10.1017/9781009587143

First published 2025

A catalogue record for this publication is available from the British Library

ISBN 978-1-009-58718-1 Hardback
ISBN 978-1-009-58716-7 Paperback
ISSN 2976-5684 (online)
ISSN 2976-5676 (print)

Cambridge University Press & Assessment has no responsibility for the persistence or accuracy of URLs for external or third-party internet websites referred to in this publication and does not guarantee that any content on such websites is, or will remain, accurate or appropriate.

For EU product safety concerns, contact us at Calle de José Abascal, 56, 1°, 28003 Madrid, Spain, or email eugpsr@cambridge.org

Hegel and Colonialism

Elements in the Philosophy of Georg Wilhelm Friedrich Hegel

DOI: 10.1017/9781009587143
First published online: September 2025

Daniel James
Technische Universität Dresden

Franz Knappik
University of Bergen

Author for correspondence: Franz Knappik, franz.knappik@uib.no

Abstract: This Element offers the first comprehensive study of Hegel's views on European colonialism. In surprisingly detailed discussions scattered throughout much of his mature oeuvre, Hegel offers assessments that legitimise colonialism in the Americas, the enslavement of Africans, and British rule in India. The Element reconstructs these discussions as being held together by a systematic account of colonialism as racial domination, underpinned by central elements of his philosophy and situated within long-overlooked contexts, including Hegel's engagement with British abolitionism and Scottish four-stages theories of social development. Challenging prevailing approaches in scholarship, James and Knappik show that Hegel's accounts of issues like freedom, personhood, and the dialectic of lordship and bondage are deeply entangled with his disturbing views on colonialism, slavery, and race. Lastly, they address Hegel's ambivalent legacy, examining how British idealists and others adopted his pro-colonial ideas, while thinkers like C.L.R. James and Angela Davis transformed Hegel for anti-colonial purposes. This title is also available as open access on Cambridge Core.

Keywords: G.W.F. Hegel, colonialism, slavery, master-slave dialectic, anticolonialism

© Daniel James and Franz Knappik 2025

ISBNs: 9781009587181 (HB), 9781009587167 (PB), 9781009587143 (OC)
ISSNs: 2976-5684 (online), 2976-5676 (print)

Contents

1 Introduction   1

2 Hegel and Colonialism in the Americas   11

3 Hegel, Africa, and Transatlantic Slavery   19

4 Hegel and British India   34

5 The "Absolute Right" to Colonise   44

6 Conclusion: Hegel and His Legacy   56

    References   64

1 Introduction

1.1 "For Europeans, the World Is Round"

In one of his lectures on the Philosophy of History at the University of Berlin during the winter term of 1822/1823, Hegel explained to his students how he viewed the position of modern Europe within the broader context of world history. For him, European societies are underpinned by a universalist understanding of freedom deriving from Christianity: not only one tyrant or some privileged citizens, but all humans as such are entitled to live in freedom. Insofar as such freedom is realised in the institutions of modern European societies, history has come to an end: "Up to now, the periods [of world history] involved relating to an earlier and a later world-historical people. But now, with the Christian religion, the principle of the world is complete; the day of judgment has dawned for it".[1]

This means not only that no further world-historical period is to be expected *after* that of modern Europe but also that nothing in the contemporary world really lies *outside* of modern Europe:

> The Christian world, as this completion in itself, can have a link to the outside world only in a relative manner, and the point of this relationship is merely to make it manifest that the outside world is intrinsically overcome. ... The Christian world has circumnavigated the globe, dominates it[.] <For Europeans, the world is round, and what is not yet dominated is either not worth the effort or yet destined to be dominated.>[2]

At a purely descriptive level, Hegel has a point: European colonialism – the conquest, settlement, and exploitation of overseas territories undertaken by many European countries between the fifteenth and twentieth centuries – was indeed a global phenomenon. When Hegel was born in 1770, large parts of the Americas, as well as significant territories in Africa and Asia (including large areas such as the Cape Colony, British Bengal, and the Dutch East Indies), were under the rule of Spain, Portugal, Britain, France, the Netherlands, and Denmark. By the time Hegel was giving his lectures, the USA (1783), Haiti (1804), Mexico (1810), Argentina (1810), Brazil (1822), and most other parts of Latin America had won independence. Still, except for Haiti, these countries would remain dominated by their white European-descended populations, and some would maintain slavery for decades to come (the USA until 1865, Brazil until 1888). Moreover, three further waves of European colonisation were underway during Hegel's lifetime: in Australasia, where the first British colony

---

[1] LPhW 463/GW 27.1:397[10–12].
[2] GW 27.1:397[20]–398[1], cf. LPhW 463f. Part in <>: transcript von Griesheim.

in Australia was established in 1788; in Africa, where the French invaded Algiers in 1830 and used it as a basis for conquering the inner parts of Algeria, anticipating the later Scramble for Africa; and in Asia, where the British East India Company was expanding its control over the entire Indian subcontinent, Napoleon tried to turn Egypt into a French colony (Campaign in Egypt and Syria, 1798–1801), and Britain responded by extending its colonial ambitions to Central Asia and the Middle East.

Yet, in the passage from the lectures on the Philosophy of History Hegel does not merely point to the global and expansive nature of European colonialism. He also presents colonial rule and expansion as inevitable destiny and even celebrates colonialism as a world-historical process that has brought the world closer to its goal. This is appalling but also puzzling. If freedom is a universal entitlement of all human beings, according to the conception that Hegel approvingly ascribes to Christianity, how can he see anything but a complete historical disaster in the fact that, for several centuries, Europeans brought violent death, lasting oppression and exploitation, forced labour, land theft, and cultural destruction to countless people all over the world, and the forced embarcation on slave ships to more than 10.6 million Africans (counting only the documented cases[3])? Why would Hegel not instead follow the example of others such as Diderot, Kant, and Herder[4] and develop a philosophical critique of colonialism? If Hegel indeed thinks that being ruled by Europeans is the 'destiny' of non-European people, how does this influence his ongoing relevance to social and political philosophy, where his thought remains a subject of significant exegetical and theoretical interest?

To answer such questions, it is necessary to better understand Hegel's views about European colonialism, which is the undertaking of this Element.

1.2 Debating Hegel's Views on Colonialism

Much of the existing literature on Hegel's views about colonialism focuses on his treatment of "colonisation" in §248 of *Elements of the Philosophy of Right*. After discussing maritime trade in the previous section, Hegel goes on to argue as follows: "This extended link also supplies the means necessary for *colonisation* – whether sporadic or systematic – to which the fully developed civil society is driven, and by which it provides part of its population with a return to the family principle in a new country, and itself with a new market and sphere of industrial activity".[5]

As becomes more apparent from lecture transcripts, "systematic" colonisation is driven and controlled by the metropolitan government and has the

---

[3] www.slavevoyages.org/voyage/database#statistics.   [4] Cf. Muthu (2003).   [5] PhR §248.

advantage that the colonisers remain connected to the metropole (presumably, Hegel has trade and taxes in mind). "Sporadic" colonisation lacks this advantage since it occurs when individuals migrate to a foreign colony.[6] The "fully developed civil society" is "driven" to colonisation because, without state regulation, overproduction crises create poverty: contingent fluctuations in demand can easily result in overproduction, leading to excess labour supply in a given sector. As it is difficult for specialised labourers to switch professions, such imbalances can lead to unemployment, the central cause of poverty in civil society.[7] Hegel thinks that when unemployment and poverty become widespread in civil society, colonies can serve as economic and social safety valves, as they allow impoverished citizens to acquire land for agriculture and create new markets for the metropole. (He formulates these points as general observations, but his listeners would have linked them to ongoing debates about German emigration. A particularly massive emigration wave following the famine in 1816 – the 'year without a summer' – aroused political interest in emigration as a social question, including a proposal by *Bundestag* delegate Hans von Gagern in favour of state-organised emigration and colonial settlements.[8])

Commentators disagree whether Hegel's account of colonisation in PhR §248 and related texts is (a) merely descriptive,[9] or whether it also contains an evaluation. In the latter case, some hold that Hegel's comments are (b) in support of colonisation – recommending it as a remedy for overpopulation and overproduction,[10] and thus taking a stance in an ongoing debate about the economic and social utility of the colonies which involved thinkers like Smith, Steuart, Sismondi, and Malthus.[11] Others – especially authors reading Hegel as a proto-Marxist critic of capitalism – think that PhR §248 is (c) critical of colonialism: by interpreting it as a necessary consequence of civil society, Hegel meant to criticise the latter.[12]

While we find it hard to see how the relevant texts support reading (c), we do not aim to decide here between the different readings of PhR §248. As part of Hegel's theory of civil society, the account of colonisation in PhR §248 and related texts is formulated from a methodological viewpoint that, much like the contemporary economic debate on colonialism, is exclusively concerned with the domestic social and economic order. Questions about the place of European colonialism in global history and how colonial enterprises relate to the interests

---

[6] GW 26.3:1394$^{15\text{-}22}$; cf. LNP 217/GW 26.1:144^{36}–145^{8}; GW 26.2:756^{34}–757^{2}. [7] PhR §243.
[8] Moltmann (1979); Paquette (2012: 299).   [9] Wood (1990: 248); Narváez León (2019: 19).
[10] Serequeberhan (1989); Pradella (2014).
[11] Waszek (1988: 203); Paquette (2012); Pradella (2014).
[12] Hirschman (1976); Narváez León (2019: 173f.); cf. also Harvey (1981); Brennan (2014: 94).

and rights of the colonised are irrelevant to that perspective. But this does not mean that Hegel did not address questions of the latter kind, too. We only need to turn to other parts of Hegel's mature system to find texts relevant to the normative and historical assessment of European colonialism. These include the accounts of international law and world history in the *Elements of the Philosophy of Right* (or *Philosophy of Right*, for short) and *Encyclopedia*; the discussions on non-European continents and their inhabitants in the lectures on the Philosophy of History and the Philosophy of Subjective Spirit; and the treatment of slavery in the *Philosophy of Right* and various lectures.

In this study, we will focus on these latter aspects: Hegel's normative and historical assessment of European colonialism in its relationship to the colonised groups. In doing so, we build on the work of several scholars who have explored Hegel's views about colonialism beyond the economic account in PhR §248.[13] Authors like Serequeberhan (1989), Dussel (1995), Guha (2003), Pradella (2014), and Habib (2017) have pointed to the importance of Hegel's account of world history in PhR §§341–360, and in particular of his notion of an "absolute right" in PhR §§347 and 350, for the issue of colonialism (cf. Section 5). Others have focused on Hegel's relation to transatlantic slavery[14] and his views about the colonisation of the Americas.[15] In her influential 2020 article "Hegel and Colonialism", Alison Stone examines how pro-colonialist and pro-slavery strands in Hegel's texts are systematically connected with his theory of freedom – and hence, with a part of his thought that is usually seen as both central to his system, and of continued philosophical interest.

All these authors approach Hegel through a critical lens. They seek a better understanding of elements in Hegel's philosophy that they see as favouring European colonialism and, therefore, as profoundly mistaken. Others have taken a more apologetic stance. Thus, Timothy Brennan reads Hegel as a thinker who challenged Enlightenment Eurocentrism,[16] and whose analysis of civil society entails the illegitimacy of slavery.[17] In response to apparently

---

[13] On Hegel's views and legacies in matters of colonialism and race cf. most recently also the contributions in the themed issue on "Racism and Colonialism in Hegel's Philosophy", *Hegel Bulletin*, vol. 45, issues 1 and 2 (2024), and the talks in our series *Hegel (anti)kolonial* (hegelantikolonial.wordpress.com).

[14] Binder (1989); Tavarès (1992); Buck-Morss (2000). Buck-Morss and (more cautiously) Tavarès read Hegel's 1807 dialectic of lordship and bondage as commenting on the Haitian Revolution. In Buck-Morss's version, this reading has attracted much attention, even though it lacks textual evidence. It has also been criticised – convincingly in our view – by other scholars, e.g., Renault (2021), who stresses that Hegel's master–servant hierarchy is established, not overcome, by the struggle to the death. Buck-Morss's suggestion (2000: 857) that Hegel only subsequently became more conservative on issues of slavery and race is contradicted by sketches of a hierarchical view of race in writings from the Jena period: James & Knappik (2023: 101).

[15] Gerbi ([1955]2000); Hoffheimer (2001). [16] Brennan (2014: 107). [17] Ibid. (102).

racist and pro-slavery statements, Brennan points to philological issues[18] and the prejudices of Hegel's time.[19]

Hence, Hegel's views about colonialism have received a fair amount of scholarly attention, and there are different views about his normative stance on colonialism. But much of this discussion has proceeded piecemeal, interrogating quite limited selections of his texts. What is missing from the literature – and what we aim to provide in this Element – is a systematic interpretation that examines and contextualises the various discussions of colonial phenomena found in Hegel's mature texts. We reconstruct his accounts of topics like the extermination of peoples and cultures in the Americas, American societies during and after colonial rule, Jesuit missions, transatlantic slavery and its abolition, and British rule in India. We connect these accounts to relevant debates in Hegel's time and his own underlying philosophical views on issues like person- and statehood, the dialectic of lordship and bondage, and the nature of world history.

Methodologically, we thus fully embrace Stone's emphasis on the systematic connections between Hegel's views on colonialism and other, including more popular, parts of his thought, and we agree with Brennan that it is important to contextualise Hegel in the intellectual climate of his time. We also share Brennan's concern for philological issues (cf. Section 1.6). Yet, as will become apparent throughout this Element, we have found that scrutiny of Hegel's critically edited texts in their historical and systematic context yields a picture in which he develops philosophical justifications for colonial conquest and rule and even for transatlantic slavery, as a means for promoting the realisation of freedom on a global scale – necessary means, Hegel thinks, because the autonomous development of non-European groups is limited by alleged racial characteristics (cf. Section 1.4).

We do not wish to deny that Hegel's oeuvre may nevertheless be a fruitful resource for contemporary philosophy, including anti-racist and anti-colonial thought (cf. Section 6.3). But we do think that there is an urgent need for Hegel scholarship and neo-Hegelian thought to examine how Hegel's views on such topics as freedom, history, agency, personhood, and the dialectic of lordship and bondage are entangled with his positions on issues like colonial rule, race, and transatlantic slavery. If these entanglements are overlooked, and Hegel's philosophy is discussed as if it were unrelated to issues like hierarchical views of race, colonialism, and transatlantic slavery – or even fundamentally opposed to them[20] – we risk inheriting Hegel's mistakes while adopting his insights.

---

[18] Ibid. (98).   [19] Ibid. (107). Cf. also McCarney (2012: 150f.).

[20] E.g., McCarney (2012: 141); Brennan (2014); Westphal (2017: 265, 271f.); Bourke (2023: xif., 180); and even the otherwise critical discussion in Pinkard (2017: 162f.).

But is looking for a conception of colonialism in Hegel's texts even legitimate? Why should he have taken much notice of, or had more than very superficial knowledge about, other European countries' colonies in remote parts of the globe? Before examining his views on this topic, we must clarify Hegel's epistemic position vis-à-vis colonialism.

1.3 Colonial Echoes in Germany

The German-speaking countries had no overseas territories of their own during Hegel's lifetime, after Brandenburg-Prussia had sold in 1721 the last of its possessions on the African West coast (one of which Hegel mentions in a lecture[21]) and before Germany began to conquer its colonial empire in 1884. Still, the colonies were not far from people's minds in Hegel's Germany. German novels and dramas of the time, as well as popular travelogues, contributed to creating a colonial imaginary.[22] German readers had every reason to follow the coverage in newspapers and magazines[23] of the American wars of independence, the Haitian Revolution, and ongoing manoeuvres of colonial expansion, as they were crucial for relations among European nations. Earlier periods of colonial history were covered in school and university teaching and popular literature; Hegel could find accounts of the cruelty of the Spanish conquest of South America in the textbook on universal history by Johann Matthias Schröckh that he praises in an early diary entry[24] as well as in Joachim Heinrich Campe's *Die Entdeckung von Amerika* (3 vols., 1781 f.), a youth book that he cites as a student.[25]

There were also academic and public controversies in Germany that pertained to colonialism. Philosophers like Kant and Herder followed in the footsteps of Enlightenment authors abroad, such as Diderot, and argued against the legitimacy of colonial conquest.[26] Others suggested already in the late eighteenth and early nineteenth centuries – also in the context of the debates on emigration mentioned in Section 1.2 – that German countries should again have colonies.[27] German abolitionists such as Matthias Christian Sprengel and Therese Huber translated and published contributions from the French and British debates on the abolition of the slave trade – in the case of Huber in a newspaper, the *Morgenblatt für gebildete Stände*, which Hegel read at least during some periods of his life.[28] Controversies surrounded early 'scientific' versions of hierarchical views on race, which were proposed by authors like Kant and Christoph Meiners, opposed by others such as Herder and Georg

---

[21] GW 27.3:837$^{15f.}$.   [22] Zantop (1997).   [23] Such as *Minerva*, cf. Buck-Morss (2000).
[24] GW 1:3$^{14\text{-}19}$.   [25] GW 1:75^{19}.   [26] Muthu (2003).   [27] Fenske (1991).
[28] Cf. his excerpts in GW 22.

Forster, and explicitly used by Meiners to defend colonial slavery.[29] Hegel owned a copy of Meiners's 1785 *Grundriß der Geschichte der Menschheit*, which includes a summary of Meiners's theory of race. He was likely familiar with Forster's and Herder's critiques as well: he refers to a text in which Forster explicitly criticises hierarchical views of race,[30] and in his copy of the 1817 *Encyclopedia*, he noted excerpts from the very parts of *Ideas for a Philosophy of the History of Mankind* where Herder rejects the race concept.[31]

Besides, Hegel regularly read British periodicals – *Morning Chronicle*, *Edinburgh Review*, and *Quarterly Review* – that reported on topics such as the abolition debates[32] and the discussions on India, and he was familiar with various British and French books that discussed colonialism in detail. As a private teacher in Switzerland, he studied the monumental *Histoire des deux Indes* (1770),[33] a comprehensive, multivolume account of the past and present of European colonialism, edited by the Abbé Raynal and co-authored by Diderot.[34] In the same period, Hegel studied works by Scottish Enlightenment authors such as Adam Smith, Adam Ferguson, and James Steuart, which, too, contained detailed discussions of topics like colonial economy and slavery[35] – as did the works of British and French national economists whom he read later on, e.g., Sismondi.[36] As we shall argue in Section 3, Hegel was even familiar with a major work on slavery and the slave trade by a British abolitionist. Finally, Hegel closely followed the then-emerging orientalist literature.[37] Such literature contained not only scholarship on the ancient Asian cultures but also racial commentary on the contemporary mores in those countries and information about colonial rule.

Hegel apparently was quite eager to use sources like these to keep himself informed about what he himself regularly referred to as the "colonies" or "colonisation". As we will see in Sections 2 to 4, he offers fairly detailed comments and discussions about colonialism and its aftermath in the Americas, transatlantic slavery, and India under Company rule. He was also aware of further (neo)colonial activities of European powers around the globe: he mentions British trade representations in South America,[38] which were part of an attempt to develop hegemony over newly independent countries like Argentina; Lord Elphinstone's mission to Afghanistan (1808/1809),[39] which prepared British expansion in Central Asia; and British settlements in

---

[29] Meiners (1790). [30] GW 2:283[26], referring to Forster (1789: xxxvi–xlii).
[31] James & Knappik (2023: 118). [32] Dumas (2017). [33] Rosenkranz (1844: 60).
[34] The library of Hegel's employer in Tschugg contained a 1775 reprint of the second edition (1774): Schneider (1997: 311).
[35] Waszek (1988). [36] Pradella (2014).
[37] Rathore & Mohapatra (2017); Said ([1978]2019: 77–79 and passim).
[38] GW 26.3:1401[38f.]. [39] GW 27.4:1290[26–33].

Australia.[40] Michelet's edition of the lectures on the Philosophy of History reports both a prediction that Europeans would eventually colonise also China,[41] and a (seemingly endorsing) reference to the 1830 conquest of Algiers mentioned in Section 1.1.[42] The Hegelian corpus thus echoes all the major colonial developments in Hegel's lifetimes invoked in Section 1.1.

1.4 Hegel on European Colonialism as Racial Domination

Not only was Hegel very much aware of the history and present state of European colonialism, but arguably also viewed it as distinct from *ancient* colonisation. As will emerge in the course of this Element, his discussions are held together by an implicit conception that identifies a fundamental characteristic of European colonialism, namely, its character as *racial domination*. European rule over the Americas, the enslavement of Africans, and British rule in India are all described by Hegel as forms of violence and domination that one racial group, Europeans, exercises over other racial groups.[43] For Hegel, these various colonial regimes are assessed in terms of a 'liberating' or 'civilising' function (cf. Section 5), and this function depends for its efficacy on forms of domination that are 'adequate' to the racial characteristics Hegel ascribes to the colonised.

By connecting colonial rule to race, this implicit conception captures a crucial feature which indeed sets apart modern European from ancient colonialism: the massive extent to which it was linked to processes of racialisation and corresponding racist ideologies. Yet, at the same time, Hegel arguably fully endorses the pro-colonialist implications and racist underpinnings of this modern form of colonialism. Indeed, as will become clear throughout this Element, Hegel's discussions of colonialism rely at crucial junctures on his own hierarchical account of race. We have elsewhere reconstructed this account as an application of basic notions from Hegel's metaphysics to the phenomenon of human diversity:[44] Hegel considers it metaphysically necessary that human spirit is realised, at least temporarily, through different, group-specific, and geographically located levels of mental ability. These levels range from a mere capacity – which he ascribes to people of African origin[45] – for being

---

[40] PhH 136/GW 27.4:1204^{15f}.

[41] PhH 207/SW 12:179; only a few years later, Britain launched the First Opium War against China (1839–1842).

[42] "This part [of Africa] was to be – *must* be attached to Europe", PhH 150/SW 12:121; cf. Pradella (2014: 444).

[43] Ethnicity or 'national spirit' plays a role in Hegel's argument, too, esp. when it comes to British India; but for Hegel, the British and Indian ethnicities are just further specifications of the European and Asian races, cf. Section 4.4.

[44] James & Knappik (2023).   [45] GW 25.1:35^{26}, 36$^{3-5}$, cf. PhSG 2:53-55; Section 3.4.

taught abstract thought and rational behaviour by others, to a limited form of intelligence that he assigns to Asians,[46] and finally, to the fully rational cognitive and volitional abilities he claims for Europeans.[47] The Indigenous peoples of America and Oceania are seen as a contingent addition to this scheme, with Americans ranking even lower than Africans.[48] Importantly, Hegel considers these racial characteristics to be hereditary,[49] but not unchangeable. Instead, he speculates that acquired traits can gradually become innate[50] – an assumption that, as we will see, undergirds Hegel's contention that colonialism and slavery gradually 'educate' racial groups who had hitherto been considered mentally inferior to Europeans.

1.5 Overview of the Following Sections

Sections 2–4 examine Hegel's comments on concrete forms of colonial regimes in the Americas and India. Section 2 addresses the colonial and postcolonial Americas, focusing on four central topics in Hegel's discussions: differences between the British colonisation of North America and the Spanish colonisation of Latin America; the mass killings and cultural destruction of Indigenous American people; the structure of colonial and postcolonial societies in Britain's Thirteen Colonies/the USA and Spanish America; and the Jesuit missions in Latin America, the so-called 'reductions'.

In Section 3, we turn to transatlantic slavery. Taking our cue from a section in Hegel's *Philosophy of Right* that presents views for and against the legitimacy of slavery as forming an "antinomy", we uncover the hitherto ignored connections of this text to the contemporary abolitionist debate in Great Britain. We locate Hegel's own discussion of slavery and abolition in the context of this debate and reconstruct the philosophical basis of Hegel's qualified justification of slavery in his theory of personhood and property and the dialectic of lordship and bondage.

In Section 4, we discuss Hegel's comments on British rule in India. By interpreting Hegel's remarks against the background of his sources and the contemporary British debates about colonial policy in India, we argue that Hegel favours the East Indian Company's initial attitude of (strategically motivated) toleration vis-à-vis traditional Indian cultures and societies against those who were campaigning for a more assimilationist approach. Unlike in the cases of Americans and Africans, Hegel does ascribe, in our reading, personhood and rights to people in India. Nevertheless, he has no objections to British rule and even explicitly postulates a civilising mission of the British.

---

[46] Cf. Section 4.4.   [47] GW 25.1:37$^{23-37}$, cf. PhSG 2:61.   [48] Cf. Hoffheimer (2001).
[49] Ibid.; James & Knappik (2023).
[50] PhSG 2:91/GW 25.1:244^{21}-245^3, cf. James & Knappik (2023: 107f.).

In Section 5, we explore the normative framework that allows Hegel to legitimise not only the colonisation of America and the enslavement of Africans but also colonial rule in the cases where his theory of race yields slightly less derogatory results, such as India. To do so, we offer a reading of Hegel's comments on the "absolute right of the Idea" in the final part of the *Philosophy of Right*. We identify a hitherto neglected background to this notion in the Scottish Enlightenment, particularly its 'four-stages theories' of social development. This context enables us to argue that Hegel's account of the "absolute right" carries pro-colonial implications and serves to justify European rule in Asia, too.

Section 6 concludes by putting Hegel's discussions of colonialism into broader historical perspective. After locating Hegel vis-à-vis Enlightenment critiques of colonialism and emerging liberal imperialism, we offer a brief overview of his deeply ambivalent legacy in matters of colonialism and slavery.

In his discussions of colonialism, race, and ethnicity, Hegel orders immensely complex human, cultural and historical realities along highly generic lines of division, grouping together the inhabitants and societies of entire continents under artificial labels defined by prejudiced 'characteristics'. This style of thinking is itself a typical feature of colonial discourse and Enlightenment racism.[51] As we are reconstructing Hegel's discussions on colonialism, our exposition follows the way he divides phenomena; however, we ask readers to bear in mind that we do not thereby endorse those divisions, let alone the labels he attaches to them.

1.6 A Note on the Texts

Hegel's most detailed discussions of the European colonies are found in lectures on the Philosophy of History, Subjective Spirit and Right he gave during his time in Berlin (1818–1831). Most older editions of these lectures, still widely used in Hegel scholarship, are philologically opaque compilations of various transcripts and manuscripts. Meanwhile, the extant transcripts have been published in critical editions in the authoritative academy edition, *Gesammelte Werke* (GW). In this Element, we use GW as the principal source for the lectures.[52] Many of these transcripts remain untranslated. Where transcripts coincide with the text in older editions of which there are translations, we use those; where no translation is available, we provide our own.

---

[51] Said ([1978]2019: 227 and passim); Andrade (2017: 306f.).
[52] For further discussion, cf. James & Knappik (2023: 101f.).

2 Hegel and Colonialism in the Americas

2.1 The Violence of Colonisation

An important part of traditional colonial discourse consists in the notion that the colonisation of North America, especially when undertaken by the British, essentially differed from how Latin, and particularly Spanish, America was colonised. On this account, which has its roots in the anti-Spanish 'Black Legend' of the sixteenth and seventeenth centuries,[53] Spanish colonisation took the form of *conquest*, marked by brutality, mass murder (as documented in early reports by authors like Bartolomé de las Casas),[54] and the subjugation of Indigenous populations to the Spanish crown, and driven by motives such as greed for silver and gold, a lust for domination or 'spirit of conquest',[55] as well as Catholic fanaticism.[56] By contrast, British colonisation was depicted as a largely peaceful process of settlement *between* Indigenous territories, driven by meaningful purposes such as agriculture and commerce. This process created new settler societies, characterised by protestant tolerance, alongside independent Indigenous nations,[57] and was beneficial for the native Americans, too.[58]

While of limited historical accuracy – British colonisation, too, involved warfare, a mentality of conquest and lust for riches[59] – this account was politically convenient for Britain and became hugely influential.[60] Hegel could read versions of it in various authors he was familiar with[61] and adopted it himself when structuring the discussions of the Americas in his courses on the Philosophy of History around the contrast between Spanish colonies in South America and British colonies in North America.[62] (Like his account of Africa, he relegates these discussions to the introductory part on the "geographical basis of world history", as he thought Indigenous Americans and Africans had never entered world history; cf. Section 3.4.) Hegel points out that the Spanish "have conquered South America in order to rule, in order to get rich".[63] North America, by contrast, has been "populated" (*bevölkert*)[64] by Europeans who

---

[53] Pagden (1995: 62–102, 185); Elliott (2006: 9); Greer et al. (2008). [54] Pagden (1995: 87).
[55] Ibid. (71). [56] Ibid. (43, 65, 69). [57] Ibid. (185). [58] Ibid. (68, 84–88).
[59] Elliott (2006: 9, 15). [60] Pagden (1995: 87).
[61] These include Montesquieu ([1748]1995: X 5, 1:305; XXI 21, 2:691f.), Smith ([1776]1999: 2:144f., 166–169), and Raynal/Diderot (Pagden 1995: 166–168).
[62] Hegel offers little discussion of the other American colonies, incl. those in the Caribbean; but cf. footnote 214 on the Haitian Revolution.
[63] GW 27.4:1210^4, cf. PhH 139.
[64] GW 27.4:1210^9, PhG 60. The older editions have "colonised" (*kolonisiert*: PhH 139/SW 12:111), which leads Paquette (2012: 300) to suppose that Hegel restricts 'colonisation' (also in PhR §248) terminologically to "a peaceful process of encroachment and settlement without expropriation". But this is not supported by the critical editions; cf. also Hegel's comments on violent colonisation in North America cited in the next paragraph.

settled in the "neighbourhood" of Indigenous people,[65] bought land from them, and assigned new territories to them; warfare was used only by Indigenous groups in their conflicts with each other.[66]

Hegel's comments on the American colonies thus echo long-standing ideological notions. Yet, against this foil, it is also possible to identify more original views in his discussions. In particular, his comments on the mass killings of Indigenous populations and the destruction of their cultures cut across the traditional contrast between Spanish conquest and British settlement. While that tradition acknowledges such violence only in the case of the *conquistadores*, Hegel stresses that the colonisation of North America, too, has had an enormous human toll. The peoples of North America, he tells his students, have "gradually vanished":[67] "The original inhabitants have been as good as annihilated by the immigrants and only continue to exist in small tribes".[68]

Rather than blaming the colonisers for their violence, however, Hegel tends to mystify that violence and depict it as a spontaneous process, an automatic decline and "disappearance" of American peoples due to their mere spatial vicinity to the European colonisers: "In the contact with more educated peoples, with more intense education, these weakly educated peoples have disappeared".[69] In the case of the British colonies in North America, he even talks about a "wondrously annihilating effect" that the mere "neighbourship of the Europeans" had upon them.[70] Indigenous peoples were, he contends, "attacked by the alien European culture as by a poison and overcome by it".[71]

Hegel uses the same rhetoric when it comes to the cultural impact of colonialism. He explicitly acknowledges that European colonisation destroyed Indigenous cultures: "the conquest was the ruin of this [American] culture".[72] "Mexico and Peru", he points out, "had reached the most significant levels of culture".[73] Yet, these and other American cultures could not resist the Europeans: "The old American world has disappeared".[74]

Hegel is well aware that all this did not occur magically but had concrete causes: he points to the technological and military inferiority of Indigenous Americans – their lack of "horse and iron"[75] – as well as the introduction of liquor in North America and the role of imported diseases.[76] But why does Hegel then foreground the picture of a process of 'disappearing', rhetorically

---

[65] GW 27.4:1205^{16}. [66] GW 27.3:822$^{33-36}$. [67] PhH 136/GW 27.4:1205^{17}.
[68] PhSG 2:63/GW 25.1:232^{28}-233^2.
[69] GW 27.2:510$^{5-7}$, cf. LPhS 90/GW 25.2:611$^{2-4}$; Hoffheimer (2001: 36).
[70] GW 27.4:1205$^{19f.}$. [71] GW 27.3:822$^{11f.}$. [72] GW 27.2:509$^{20f.}$.
[73] GW 27.4:1204$^{20f.}$, cf. PhH 136. [74] GW 27.3:822^7.
[75] PhH 137/GW 27.2:510^{16}, a notion already found in Montaigne: Gerbi ([1955]2000: 592n.).
[76] Liquor: PhH 136/ GW 27.4:1205^{22}; diseases: GW 27.4:1205^{22}.

downplaying the agency of the colonisers who were responsible for large-scale cultural and biological extermination?

The reason for this can be found in his views about the geographic and racial characteristics of the Americas and their Indigenous inhabitants. Building on a strand of colonial discourse that goes back to Buffon and includes seminal works like de Pauw's *Recherches philosophiques sur les Américains* (1768) and the *Histoire des deux Indes* (1770),[77] Hegel thinks the New World is generally defined by weakness and immaturity – a "young, weak country".[78] Not only are New World animals smaller and weaker than their Old World counterparts,[79] but humans, too, are of a "weaker species" [*Geschlecht*][80] in America. This "inferiority" is not only a matter of physical constitution – e.g., small body size – but also of "spiritual", i.e., psychological and cultural, characteristics.[81] Thus, Indigenous Americans, Hegel thinks, display a "mild and passionless disposition, want of spirit, and a crouching submissiveness toward a Creole, and still more toward a European".[82] Similarly, traditional culture in the Americas, including that of the Incas, Mayas, and Aztecs, was "of a feebler stock".[83] Indeed, the lack of horses and iron among Americans is itself an expression of this characteristic American weakness.[84]

Hence, Hegel's choice of the terms in which he depicts biological and cultural mass destruction in the colonial Americas suggests that these phenomena were a direct consequence, not so much of the aggressiveness of the Europeans but of the typically American weakness that fundamentally characterises life – organic, mental, and cultural – in the New World. Hegel does not explicitly evaluate the extermination of Indigenous cultures and populations, but this silence is in itself telling, given not only how common it was in writings of his time to denounce the lethal side of colonialism, at least in South America, but also that he elsewhere in the lectures on the Philosophy of History does seem to voice his disapproval of reported instances of ethnic killing[85] and the desecration of local religious symbols.[86]

Overall, Hegel's comments convey an account of colonial extermination in the Americas that can be seen as inverting a crucial element of the Black Legend. The latter sees colonial violence on the part of the *conquistadores* as an expression of negative racial features ascribed to the *perpetrators* as Spaniards (due to their partially Islamic heritage, the Black Legend treats Spanish people as Black and

---

[77] Cf. Gerbi ([1955]2000).   [78] GW 27.2:509^{21}.   [79] GW 27.4:1205$^{1-4}$.
[80] PhSG 2:63/GW 25.1:232^{18}.   [81] PhH 137/GW 27.4:1206$^{10f., 33}$.
[82] PhH 136/GW 27.4:1206$^{7f.}$.   [83] LPhW 192/GW 27.1:79^{4}.
[84] PhH 137/GW 27.4:1204$^{23-26}$.   [85] PhH 270/SW 12:244, cf. GW 27.2:616$^{27f.}$.
[86] PhH 397/SW 12:374, cf. GW 27.2:719$^{26f.}$.

African).[87] For Hegel, by contrast, such violence responds to the negative racial features he ascribes to the *victims* qua Indigenous Americans. As we will see throughout this Element, the notion that determinate forms of colonial violence match or are 'appropriate' to the alleged racial features of particular groups is a guiding thread in Hegel's views on colonialism.

2.2 American (Post)Colonial Societies

Besides the exterminatory effects of conquest and settlement, Hegel discusses the structure and development of colonial societies in the Americas, including the recent and ongoing independence processes. In the case of the Thirteen Colonies/USA, Hegel paints, consistently with the traditional account, a rather rosy picture of settlers who draw on the "treasure of European culture"[88] and the ethos of Protestantism[89] in their ongoing efforts of expansion[90] and development of agriculture, trade, and commerce.[91] The fact that the settlers have not yet reached the boundaries of the continent means that as soon as social inequality and "discontent"[92] arise among them, the remedy of further expansion is always available. Consequently, the formation of a proper civil society in the USA – including social stratification, urbanisation, and industrialisation[93] – is still in its beginnings. Hence, there is not yet a felt "necessity for a firm combination",[94] for a robust political organisation, either. The present republican constitution of the USA only serves to protect the safety and private property of the settlers[95] and thus is, by Hegel's light, a mere "state of necessity and the understanding".[96] Further social development will make it necessary to create a more robust and organic state, perhaps a monarchy.[97]

Hegel thus can be seen as extrapolating the traditional, positive account of British colonisation into a narrative of the Thirteen Colonies/USA as a (post) colonial success story – failing almost entirely to consider what challenges the ongoing oppression of Afrodiasporic and Indigenous groups might create for the development towards an 'organic' society. He was well aware that "the Southern states are based on slavery" and dominated by the planter aristocracy ("nobility"),[98] knew about ongoing debates on abolition in the USA,[99] and

---

[87] Fuchs (2008: 94–98); Hegel seems to endorse this view: Enc. §394 Add., PhSG 2:75/SW 10:67.
[88] GW 27.2:512$^{2f.}$, cf. PhH 138; Smith ([1776]1999: 2:145). [89] PhH 140/GW 27.4:1211$^{2-7}$.
[90] PhH 141f./GW 27.4:1214^{11}. [91] PhH 140/GW 27.2:512$^{6-16}$.
[92] PhH 142/GW 27.4:1214^{17}.
[93] GW 27.2:512$^{10f., 13-20}$; GW 27.4:1213$^{18-22}$; cf. PhH 142. [94] PhH 141/GW 27.4:1213^{17}.
[95] PhH 140/GW 27.4:1210$^{15-18}$. [96] PhR §183. [97] LPhW 193/GW 27.1:80^{13}.
[98] GW 27.4:1215$^{17f.}$; that Hegel is discussing here slavery in the Southern USA, not in South America, is made clear by his reference to the predominance of cotton production at GW 27.4:1215^{37}.
[99] PhR §270 Rem., GW 14.1:217$^{18-21}$, probably referring to the 1819/1820 Congress debates leading to the Missouri Compromise.

echoes contemporary debates in the USA[100] by pointing out that the contrast between the slave economy of the South and the Northern states holds the potential for a civil war.[101] Still, he interprets even this as merely an issue of conflicting "interests"[102] among different groups of whites.

Hegel is much more attentive to intrinsic problems of (post)colonial societies in the case of Spanish America.[103] The Spanish colonies, he points out, stood under the twofold yoke of political despotism and the "spiritual oppression" of Catholicism.[104] Here, a society defined by race and class hierarchies emerged, where "the people" were oppressed by secular and ecclesiastic elites ("higher classes"),[105] and Indigenous Americans were dominated by Spanish-born people and a mixed-race population of "creoles" – "a mixture of European and American or African blood",[106] who "set the tone" in Latin America.[107]

Interestingly, Hegel identifies several elements that stabilise the hierarchy of colonial society, leading to a "fixed social order"[108] that resists ongoing emancipatory struggles. The first is an undue emphasis on social distinction; people are driven by "ambition" and "thirst after orders and titles".[109] They are, therefore, submissive towards those who can bestow the desired social status – the result being a general "spirit of servitude".[110] At least in the case of Spanish and Creole groups,[111] Hegel seems to consider the "spirit of servitude" a product of colonial society; it is opposed to the "noble, free" character he ascribes to the inhabitants of the metropole.[112] A second stabilising feature is Catholic "superstition", specifically the use of religious belief to defend the existing order.[113] As an illustration, Hegel mentions the Caracas earthquake in 1812, where the interpretation supplied by church authorities and Spanish royalists – a divine punishment for the independentist cause – created a drawback to the Venezuelan War for Independence.[114]

---

[100] For a possible source, cf. Tallmadge (1819: 166, 171). [101] GW 27.4:1215$^{15-17}$.
[102] GW 27.4:1215^{17}.
[103] On Hegel's account of Latin American societies and the contrast with the USA, cf. Ferreiro (2019).
[104] GW 27.3:823$^{9,\ 14}$. [105] GW 27.3:824^{19}. [106] GW 27.3:823^{21}.
[107] GW 27.2:510^{10}, cf. LPhW 193/GW 27.1:79^{12}–80^{1}. – Probably due the ambiguity of the term "creole" and limitations in his sources, Hegel fails to recognise crucial differences in the colonial *casta* system: *criollos* – American-born people of completely Spanish descent – were socially privileged if compared to *mestizos* – descendants of Spanish and Indigenous American persons – and *mulattos* – descendants of Spanish and *negros* (i.e., African-descended persons).
[108] GW 27.3:824^{24}.
[109] GW 27.3:824^{17}; cf. de Azara ([1809]1810: 359), but also more recent historical research on colonial societies in Latin America, e.g., Fragoso (2015).
[110] GW 27.3:824^{21}.
[111] On "submissiveness" as one of the main racial characteristics of Indigenous Americans, see PhH 136/GW 27.4:1206$^{7f.}$.
[112] GW 27.3:823^{14}. [113] GW 27.3:824$^{19f.}$.
[114] GW 27.3:824$^{25-28}$. The transcripts refer to an earthquake in 1809 without providing a location; the 1812 Caracas earthquake seems the only event that otherwise fits Hegel's description.

Third, and most interestingly, Hegel also cites racial hostilities in this context: the Creoles, he points out, "lived in arrogance and contempt of the Indigenous Americans – and they all are in their turn subjected to the Spanish pride".[115] The context of this passage – an account of a hierarchical social order in critical and pejorative terms – suggests that Hegel at least implicitly means to criticise such racist animus. This is remarkable, given that Hegel himself endorses a theory of race that massively denigrates non-European groups (cf. Section 1.4) and legitimises, as we will see, various forms of colonial domination. Hegel may rely here on a distinction similar to the contemporary one between 'cognitive' and 'volitional' forms or accounts of racism:[116] he may have thought that there is a difference between, on the one hand, what he framed as disinterested discussions about anthropology and colonial policy, and, on the other, overt racially motivated disdain or arrogance.[117] We will come back to related issues in Section 5.4.

In his remarks on the societies of Spanish America, Hegel thus identifies the "spirit of servitude", Catholic ideology, and racist feelings as elements that contribute to the maintenance of a strict, race-based social hierarchy. Not only has this hierarchy retarded the process of independence, as in the case of the Caracas earthquake, but Hegel suggests that it also tends to destabilise the governments of the newly independent countries. He points out that the young Latin American republics "depend only on military force; their whole history is a continued revolution".[118]

This instability shows that the "spirit of true free self-consciousness", the revolutionary spirit of the independentist movements which rebelled against the Spanish crown and the Spanish-born local elites, is "not sufficient to shake off the yoke" of Spanish domination; instead, a stable and free political order after colonialism would require "a proper education and instruction of the people".[119] Hence, Hegel indicates the need for a social and cultural transformation in postcolonial Latin American societies, which presumably would have to dismantle the existing hierarchical order by addressing dominant patterns of social reward ("spirit of servitude"), religious irrationality, and racial animosity.

Among Hegel's discussions of colonial phenomena, his remarks on South America stand out as they offer elements of a critical analysis of (post)colonial societies, which are informed by but also go beyond the traditional critique of Spanish colonialism mentioned in Section 2.1. However, despite Hegel's attention to obstacles to the independence process in South America, he does not

---

[115] GW 27.3:824[14f.]   [116] E.g., Urquidez (2020: 4f. and passim).
[117] Anti-Spanish prejudice on Hegel's side (cf. Paquette, 2012: 300 n.28) may also play a role here. (Thanks to Alison Stone for suggesting this point).
[118] PhH 139/GW 27.4:1209[22–24].   [119] GW 27.3:824[22–24].

articulate an analysis of the revolutions in North and Latin America themselves; he shows no interest in their normative basis or the political processes driving them. Indeed, it is possible to hypothesise that these revolutions had no world-historical significance for him. What was important for world history was that Europe expanded its dominion over the globe (cf. the quotes opening Section 1). Since the American revolutions, as Hegel acknowledges in the case of South America, left intact the colonial social hierarchies, they did not really change the system of global European rule.

What Hegel's assessment neglects, however, is that Indigenous American and Afrodiasporic people did play a part and pursue their own agenda in the revolutionary struggles. The North American Revolution saw hundreds of thousands of Black soldiers fighting for independence from Britain and numerous enslaved people gaining manumission. In Latin America, Indigenous people built on centuries-old traditions of anti-colonial resistance when participating in the wars of independence.[120] Despite their relevance for his account of world history, Hegel is not able to register such complexities because he postulates on racial grounds that (in the case of Latin America) only creoles, not Indigenous Americans, have been capable of reaching "the higher feeling of self, the upward-striving to autonomy, independence".[121] Even where he is aware of a potential counter-example, such as the *llaneros*, nomadic riders with Indigenous roots who live in the Orinoco grasslands and played an important role in the Venezuelan War of Independence, he is quick to explain it away as a result of European influences: the *llaneros* owe their bravery to their horses, which come from Europe.[122]

2.3 The Jesuit Reductions

Hegel's views on the Indigenous inhabitants of South America are also deeply problematic when it comes to the question of how Europeans and their descendants should treat them. Rather than immediate freedom in a transformed post-colonial society, the "best thing that can be granted"[123] to Indigenous Americans consists, Hegel claims, in the particular form of colonial regime that Jesuits (and to a minor extent Franciscans) had established in their missions in the Rio de la Plata basin (especially among the Guarani in present-day Paraguay), Mexico, and California, known as 'reductions' (*reducciónes*).[124]

The Jesuit reductions were settlements in which Jesuits lived together with Indigenous groups from surrounding areas, both to evangelise them and to

---

[120] Cf. Dussel (1995: 107–109, 126–128).   [121] GW 27.2:510$^{8f.}$.
[122] GW 27.2:510$^{15f.}$, 27.4:1206$^{5f.}$.   [123] PhSG 2:65/GW 25.1:233^{22}, translation modified.
[124] Cf. Ganson (2003).

protect them from slave raids. The first reductions were established in the early seventeenth century; they declined after the Jesuits were expelled from Spanish America in 1767. Hailed by some as utopian social experiments that used communal instead of private property and enabled Indigenous people to live in safety according to their own customs,[125] criticised by others as an oppressive 'state within the state' where Indigenous people were forced to work for the enrichment of the Jesuit order,[126] the reductions were much debated in eighteenth-century Europe and are alive in the memory of the European public in the early nineteenth century.[127] Hegel presents the reductions as highly paternalistic regimes (a "paternal government")[128] that dictated virtually all details of adult Indigenous persons' lives: They were forced to carry out agricultural work, the products of which were stored and distributed to cover the needs of subsistence.[129] The day was divided into labour and worship; bells were even rung at midnight to remind the inhabitants of sexual intercourse.[130]

Hegel considers this the "best thing that can be granted" to Indigenous Americans because he sees a perfect match between the regime of the reductions and the racial characteristics of Indigenous Americans. On his account, the weakness that characterises Indigenous Americans (cf. Section 2.1) makes them devoid of any desires and drives,[131] and hence also incapable of providing even for the immediate future.[132] Instead, Hegel cites reports according to which they "live entirely for the moment, like animals".[133] Thus, Hegel denies Indigenous Americans some of the most basic mental preconditions of human agency, arguing that by treating them like children[134] (and much worse), the Jesuits found the "most appropriate way" of assisting their development.[135]

---

[125] Cf. Montesquieu ([1748]1995: IV 6, 1:140f.); Dussel (1995: 68f).

[126] Cf. Voltaire ([1759]1969): ch. 14, 90).

[127] Thus, Hegel could read the anecdote about midnight bells (see the end of this paragraph) in an 1810 translation of *Voyage dans l'Amérique méridionale depuis 1781 jusqu'en 1801* by Félix de Azara (1746–1821) – the likely source for much of what Hegel says about the reductions (de Azara [1809]1810: 291) – but also in *Minerva* the same year (Anonymous 1810, 465). – More recent accounts, such as Ganson (2003), see the reductions as sites of Indigenous self-determination and resistance, also against Jesuit rule.

[128] PhSG 2:65/GW 25.1:233^{21}, translation modified; cf. de Azara ([1809]1810): 341).

[129] PhSG 2:65/GW 25.1:233$^{22-26}$, cf. de Azara ([1809]1810): 341).

[130] PhSG 2:65/GW 25.1:234$^{2-4}$. [131] PhH 137/GW 27.4:1206$^{18,\ 24}$.

[132] PhSG 2:65/GW 25.1:233$^{27f.}$; cf. de Azara ([1809]1810): 341). Already de Azara ([1809]1810: 342) argued that the Guanari could not actually be that child-like given that they used to live on their own before the arrival of the Jesuits, but Hegel ignores this point.

[133] PhSG 2:65/GW 25.1:233^{29}. [134] GW 27.2:511^{8}.

[135] PhSG 2:65/GW 25.1:233^{26}. By contrast, Hegel criticises the "slavery" of Indigenous Americans in Spanish America (i.e., the *repartimiento* system) as oppressive (LPhS 90/GW 25.2:611$^{26f.}$, PhH 136/GW 27.4:1205$^{24f.}$), presumably because of its more exploitative and less 'paternal' character.

Hegel's comments on the Jesuit reductions add an important side to his discussion of colonialism in South America. They make clear that Hegel's notion of a social and cultural transformation in postcolonial South America is exclusionary, as it is not meant to apply to Indigenous groups, at least not at present. At the same time, Hegel's account of the reductions is a further instance of how he sees specific forms of colonial violence as appropriate to the colonised groups' racial characteristics – and hence his view of European colonialism as racial domination. We will again find this notion in the other forms of colonial regimes discussed in the following sections, beginning with an aspect of colonialism that connects the Americas to Africa: transatlantic slavery.

3 Hegel, Africa, and Transatlantic Slavery

3.1 The 'Antinomy of Slavery'

Of all aspects of European colonialism, transatlantic slavery receives the most attention and philosophical elaboration from Hegel. He comments on it repeatedly when discussing Africa and its inhabitants in the lectures on the Philosophy of History and the Philosophy of Subjective Spirit. He also addresses this issue when he discusses the dialectic of lordship and bondage in his lectures on Subjective Spirit.[136] Yet arguably, Hegel's most prominent discussion of transatlantic slavery is found in the section on Abstract Right within his 1821 *Elements of the Philosophy of Right*. In his long Remark to §57 in this Element, Hegel presents two opposite positions regarding slavery, which, he tells us, form an "antinomy":

> [Thesis] The alleged justification of *slavery* (with all its more specific explanations in terms of physical force, capture in time of war, the saving and preservation of life, sustenance, education, acts of benevolence, the slave's own acquiescence, etc.), as well as the justification of lordship [*Herrschaft*] as simple domination [*Herrenschaft*] in general, and all *historical* views on the right of slavery and lordship, depend on regarding the human being simply as a *natural being* [*Naturwesen*] whose *existence* (of which the arbitrary will is also a part) is not in conformity with his concept.
>
> [Antithesis] Conversely, the claim that slavery is absolutely contrary to right is firmly tied to the *concept* of the human being as spirit, as something free *in itself*, and is one-sided inasmuch as it regards the human being as *by nature* free, or (and this amounts to the same thing) takes the concept as such in its immediacy, not the Idea, as the truth.[137]

---

[136] Cf. Kuch (2013: 193–196).
[137] PhR §57 Rem.; paragraph break and Kantian labels added.

Thesis and Antithesis in this antinomy thus stand for opposite evaluations of slavery: according to the Thesis, slavery is justified, while according to the Antithesis, it is illegitimate. Yet, as with all antinomies, in Hegel's view,[138] both positions are one-sided and must be integrated into a more comprehensive conception (more on this later).

Some commentators have connected §57 Remark to ancient Greece and Rome[139] and the Thesis to Aristotle's doctrine of natural slavery.[140] However, this cannot explain Hegel's detailed catalogue of justifications or "explanations" for slavery: "physical force, capture in time of war, the saving and preservation of life, sustenance, education, acts of benevolence, the slave's own acquiescence", in addition to "all *historical* views on the right of slavery".[141] None of these points matches Aristotle's views on natural slavery nor other references that have been proposed.[142] Instead, one needs to see Hegel's discussion in the context of contemporary debates on slavery in Great Britain to make sense of those details.

While there had been long-standing traditions of resistance against slavery in the British Empire – including the creation of militant maroon societies, slave rebellions, legal action (*Somerset* v. *Stewart*, 1772) and anti-slavery writing by authors such as Aphra Behn, Granville Sharp, and Anthony Benezet, only in the 1780s did there emerge a campaign in the metropole that eventually led to the 1807 ban on the slave trade.[143] One important figure in this campaign was Thomas Clarkson (1760–1846).[144] In 1785, while a student at Cambridge, Clarkson wrote a prize-winning essay against slavery and the slave trade. Subsequently, he realised that his arguments demanded action. He cofounded the Society for Effecting the Abolition of the Slave Trade in 1787 and cooperated with other white abolitionists like Sharp and William Wilberforce, as well as Black abolitionists like Ottobah Cugoano and Olaudah Equiano. Besides, he published an English translation of his Latin student essay under the title *An Essay on the Slavery and Commerce of the Human Species, Particularly the African* (1786). The text became an important document for the abolitionist movement, also internationally. It was widely reprinted, and as late as 1846, the year Clarkson died, several obituaries in German newspapers referred to him as the author of the "famous" *Essay*.[145]

---

[138] Cf. SL 158/GW 21:181$^{6-12}$. [139] Oquendo (1999). [140] Alznauer (2015), 54n.
[141] PhR §57 Rem. By "historical", Hegel seems to mean here justifications in terms of positive law. The related formulations "historical views" of "lordship" and "lordship as domination" refer to Karl Ludwig von Haller's conservative legal positivism, cf. PhR §258 Rem.
[142] E.g., Meiners: GW 14.3:1072f.
[143] On the history of abolitionism, cf. Turley (1991); Midgley (1992); Davis (1999); Matthews (2006).
[144] On Clarkson's biography, see Smith (2010: 16f., 28–41).
[145] E.g., *Frankfurter Konversationsblatt* 8.10.1846: 1112; *Bayerische Landbötin* 8.10.1846: 1024.

Table 1 Correspondences between Hegel and Clarkson

Hegel (PhR §57 Rem.)	Clarkson ([1786]2010)
"physical force"	II.5: slaves who are "collected by means of violence and oppression" (127; cf. I.2)
"capture in time of war"	I.2, II.7: enslavement of *"prisoners of war"* (78, 131; cf. I.3, 83)
"the saving and preservation of life"	I.7: justification for enslavement of prisoners of war in Roman law: "a right ... from the consideration of having saved the lives of the vanquished, when they could have taken them by the laws of war, to commute blood for service" (131; cf. II.10, 144)
"sustenance" (*Ernährung*)	II.9: "Africa is infested with locusts, and insects of various kinds; ... they settle in swarms upon the trees, destroy the verdure, consume the fruit, and deprive the inhabitants of their food." (145)
"acts of benevolence"	II.9: "You entice the Africans to war; you foment their quarrels; you supply them with arms and ammunition, and all – from the *motives of benevolence*" (144)
"education" (*Erziehung*)	III.9: "It is said that they are barbarous at home. – But do you *receivers* civilise them?" (208)
"the slave's own acquiescence"	II.10: "But you say again ... 'that they do not appear to go with you against their will.'" (145) Cf. I.1: voluntary slavery, founded on consent, as one kind of slavery (77)
"all *historical* views on the right of slavery"	II.9: "But ... if you have not even the shadow of a claim upon their persons; by what right do you receive them? 'By the laws of the Africans,' you will say; 'by which it is positively allowed.'" (143 f.)

Hegel very likely was among Clarkson's readers in Germany. For each of the items on his list of pro-slavery arguments corresponds to an argument that is presented and rebutted by Clarkson, as shown in Table 1.

In addition, Hegel's Antithesis, which "regards the human being as *by nature* free",[146] seems modelled on Clarkson's own position, which follows the natural

---

[146] PhR §57 Rem.

law tradition and holds that humans are free by birth: "*[L]iberty* is a *natural*, and *government* an *adventitious* right because all men were originally free".[147]

Within the abolitionist literature, this combination of debated arguments and claims is, as far as we can see, unique to Clarkson's *Essay*. We therefore take this comparison to show that Clarkson's *Essay* was Hegel's direct source for his antinomy of slavery.

Consequently, the discussion of slavery in §57 Rem. must be seen first and foremost in the context of transatlantic slavery. It is also worth noting that Hegel could find in Clarkson's *Essay* plenty of information about the atrocities of slavery, in addition to a spirited attack on anti-Black racism; Clarkson points to the Black poets Phillis Wheatley and Ignatius Sancho as "examples of African genius"[148] and quotes extracts from Wheatley's poems. When Hegel propagates pro-slavery positions and racist views, he does so not in ignorance but despite his knowledge of critical voices.

3.2 Resolving the 'Antinomy of Slavery'

To see why Hegel thinks both positions in the 'antinomy of slavery' are one-sided, it is helpful to consider that antinomy against the background of his more general views about freedom. Hegel's discussion of the antinomy is informed by his understanding of the kind of freedom that is, in his view, part of personhood, namely, the "personality of the will".[149] Generally speaking, freedom is not simply given for Hegel – a permanent property that a creature is either born with or forever devoid of. Instead, freedom needs to be achieved through a process of development or education. This process begins with humans as bearers of a "natural will" who cannot yet rationally control and order their drives and motives.[150] It subsequently creates the mental and social preconditions that enable humans to be guided by reason and right. For Hegel, the two sides in the antinomy correspond to two ways of understanding human existence, which both abstract away from essential parts of this process. First, if humans in their initial state of "natural beings" are taken as a paradigm, human existence is understood as "conceptless", i.e., in isolation from the essence or "concept" of humankind, which is freedom. The Thesis thus erroneously takes a mere initial phase of development as the entire truth:

> This earlier and false appearance [*Erscheinung*] is associated with the spirit which has not yet gone beyond the point of view of its consciousness; the dialectic of the concept and of the as yet only immediate consciousness of freedom gives rise at this stage to the *struggle for recognition* and the

---

[147] Clarkson ([1786]2010: II.3, 124). [148] Clarkson ([1786]2010: III.7,182). [149] PhR §39.
[150] PhR §11.

relationship of *lordship* and *servitude* (see *Phenomenology of Spirit*, pp. 115ff. and *Encyclopedia of the Philosophical Sciences*, §§325ff.).[151]

Hegel explicitly refers here to the accounts he offers in the 1807 *Phenomenology of Spirit* and the 1817 *Encyclopedia* of the dialectic of lordship and bondage, an argument that is supposed to show that a view of freedom (or 'independence') as domination is unstable and that the master–servant hierarchy necessarily gives place to more elaborate conceptions and realisations of freedom.

Second, the opposite error consists in holding fast to the essence (concept) of humans as freedom while abstracting away from its processual nature. Here, freedom is seen only as a "subjective concept", a mere ideal that is not realised because its necessary preconditions are not in place. Thus, the Antithesis claims that humans have an absolute right to be free, ignoring that such a right has to be institutionalised:

> But that the objective spirit, the content of right, should no longer be apprehended merely in its subjective concept, and consequently that the ineligibility of the human being in and for himself for slavery should no longer be apprehended merely as something which *ought* to be, is an insight which comes only when we recognise that the Idea of freedom is truly present only as *the state*.[152]

By contrast, Hegel's processual view of freedom integrates both sides. Since he rejects both the outright assertion *and* the outright denial of the legitimacy of slavery as one-sided,[153] he seems to hold that slavery is legitimate *in some qualified manner*, contextualising slavery within the process leading towards the full realisation of freedom.[154] But what does this concretely mean?

In the following, we develop an answer by examining how Hegel elaborates his position in other texts.[155] It will be useful to distinguish here between two different levels:

(a) the qualified justification of *forced labour*; as we will see, Hegel holds that *all* human groups at some point of their history go through a stage at which *some* form of forced labour is justified;

(b) the qualified justification of *the enslavement of Africans by Europeans* in transatlantic slavery, as a particular historical case of forced labour.

In Section 3.3, we reconstruct three strands of argument in Hegel's texts that speak to (a) (even though they are often formulated specifically in terms of

---

[151] PhR §57 Rem. [152] Ibid.
[153] Pace commentators like Westphal (2017: 265), who cites only the Antithesis.
[154] Cf. GW 14.2:431$^{20-22}$. [155] Cf. also Jaarte (2024).

slavery). In Section 3.4, we examine why Hegel thinks that in the case of Africans, the specific regime of enslavement by Europeans is qualifiedly justified. In the course of our discussion, we will also clarify in what sense forced labour and transatlantic slavery are "qualifiedly justified" for Hegel.

3.3 Justifying Forced Labour

1. The educational argument. In an 1822 lecture on the dialectic of lordship and bondage, Hegel argues as follows:

> All peoples had to go through the standpoint of servitude, and owe it only to the disciplining rod [*Zuchtruthe*] that a self-consciousness has awaked in them which is not the self-consciousness of mere individuality.... On the one hand, one can ... reject slavery as illegitimate; on the other hand, one can recognise it as grades of discipline [*Stufen der Zucht*].[156]

The ambivalence that Hegel ascribes to slavery here echoes the 'antinomy of slavery' introduced in Section 3.1. But Hegel also offers a concrete candidate here for an aspect of slavery that can be thought to justify slavery and, more generally, forced labour: namely, a supposed 'disciplining' or educating function.[157]

The cynical claim that forced labour has a disciplining or educating effect can already be found in the seventeenth century[158] and is part of the arguments used by the plantation lobby in the British debate around 1800.[159] It will serve as justification for forced labour well into the twentieth century, both in the context of colonialism[160] and of totalitarian regimes like Nazi Germany.[161] However, when Hegel uses this point in his lectures, he also directly builds on an element already central to the dialectic of lordship and bondage in the 1807 *Phenomenology of Spirit*. According to both the 1807 and the later versions of that dialectic, individuals who attempt to receive confirmation of their initial self-understanding as 'self-sufficient' beings – beings that everything else is subordinate to – need to go through a struggle for recognition in which they risk their life to show that nothing, not even their biological lives, has absolute value for them. Recognition occurs only once one side surrenders, leading to a hierarchical relation between a master and a servant. However, while the recognition from someone they treat as an object is worthless to the master, the servant benefits from the situation. According to the 1807 version, one reason

---

[156] GW 25.1:114$^{33-36}$, 115$^{20f.}$; cf. PhSG 3:67, 69.
[157] Cf. PhH 157/GW 27.4:1229$^{18f.}$ (translation modified): "Slavery is in and for itself unjust, for the essence of humans is freedom; but they first must become mature for it".
[158] Pagden (1995: 99).   [159] Dumas (2016: 47).   [160] Conrad (2012: 112).
[161] Buggeln & Wildt (2014).

for this lies in the 'disciplining' role of forced labour. Unlike the master, the servant is forced to control their desires: for example, they cannot simply do whatever they want since they have to work for the master, nor can they eat the fruits of their labour whenever they wish to because they need to supply them to the master. Thus, the servant "works off his natural existence"; their work is "desire *held in check*, it is vanishing *staved off*, or: work *cultivates and educates*".[162]

Both in 1807 and in later versions, the 'education' of the servant is a precondition for the subsequent development towards freedom and mutual recognition. What is new in the later texts is that Hegel explicitly applies that point to the level of human groups and their history, arguing that a stage at which societies are organised by master–servant relations is a necessary element in the development of all societies[163] (although we will see in Section 5.3 that the 1807 version already echoes debates on this topic). In addition, Hegel now uses the tools of his mature philosophy to unpack the reasons for assigning master–servant relations such a necessary role. Consider, to begin with, how Hegel continues the discussion we cited at the beginning of this subsection:

> That humans be free, this includes that their individuality be no longer natural, but that they have sublated it into the universality of their life; initially, this is the relationship in which the servant stands; he subordinates his self-sufficiency. The absolute relationship of freedom obtains when the other to which one subordinates oneself is universal ... rationality. The servant, by contrast, still subordinates himself to an individual will and has now the negative relation to himself of working away, breaking his selfish will. ... This negation has to become a habit, and this is what one calls discipline [*Zucht*].[164]

Hegel claims here that habitual subordination under someone else's will in forced labour eventually affords subjects a form of self-control they need to subordinate themselves to *social norms*. Participation in norm-governed social orders is central to ethical life and, hence, to freedom in Hegel's mature conception. At the same time, as we saw earlier, he holds that humans initially have a merely "natural will" governed by brute desires and drives – hence the need for learning self-control.[165] In the course of socio-historical development, teaching self-control eventually becomes a part of ordinary parenting practices.[166] However, at the early stages of such development, parents

---

[162] PhS ¶195. [163] Cf. also Enc. §433 Rem.
[164] GW 25.1:114^{36}–115^{10}; cf. LWPh 180/GW 27.1:65$^{2-12}$; GW 26.2:617$^{18-21}$.
[165] The initial lack of self-control also explains why individuals cannot educate themselves in this regard, and subordination to some external authority is needed in Hegel's view.
[166] GW 25.1:48$^{8-22}$, cf. PhSG 2:113.

themselves lack control over their will. Therefore, they are unable to educate others, as a capricious will does not instil respect and obedience.[167] Instead, Hegel thinks that self-control initially needs to be acquired through forced labour – where the master may themselves be stuck at a level of mere consumption of goods,[168] but the specific situation of forced labour with its need to obey, and to supply rather than consume goods (on pain of fatal violence) ensures that the servant develops abilities for self-control.

The reasoning we have reconstructed so far in this subsection amounts to a first argument that, in Hegel's view, offers a qualified justification for forced labour: freedom qua ethical life requires abilities for norm-following and hence self-control, which, in turn, presuppose disciplining processes, including a regime of forced labour as a stage of socio-historical development. Forced labour *during that phase of development* will then count as a 'necessary evil' – evil as it contradicts the human vocation for freedom but necessary as there cannot be such freedom without it.

2. Argument from personhood. A second, related strand of argument becomes visible when we consider the rights that, in Hegel's view, protect members of a free society against forced labour. These are individuals' institutionalised rights over their bodies and labour, rights that he conceptualises as *property rights* ("because the slave has no property, he is a slave").[169] However, to possess such rights, individuals must be granted them by others: they must be *recognised* as property holders. Such recognition – Hegel calls it "respect"[170] – involves leaving it up to the individuals in question to decide how they act, both with respect to the external things (*Sachen*) they own and their own lives and bodies.[171] This ability is, for Hegel, part of what it is to have a personal will, to enjoy personal freedom.[172] Moreover, for subjects to enjoy such personal freedom *safely* – independently of whether their decisions match others' interests[173] – it must be *instituted* in the form of private property rights, a norm-governed social order that constrains the will of all in accordance with their mutual recognition as property holders. Because to have a personal will just is to be a person (for Hegel), private property institutes personhood.[174] As Hegel puts it in his peculiar terminology: "Private property is the determinate being of my personality [*das Dasein meiner Persönlichkeit*]".[175]

---
[167] GW 25.1:48[16–18].   [168] Cf. PhS ¶190.   [169] GW 26.2:620[7f.]; cf. PhR §§47f., 57.
[170] PhR §36.   [171] PhR §40.   [172] Ibid.; cf. Neuhouser (2000: 24f.).
[173] Pettit (2015: 81–87).   [174] Enc. §490.
[175] Ibid. In the same section, Hegel also asserts that "[i]n property, the person is joined together [*zusammengeschlossen*] with himself". He plays on the dual meaning of the word '*schließen*', which also means 'to infer' – suggesting that human personhood depends on private property, a dependence that can be comprehended through a particular type of syllogism (*Schluss*) in which the concept of property acts as a middle term (Enc. §491). In short, personhood is mediated (*vermittelt*) by the recognition of private ownership, a recognition characteristically expressed in contract (cf. PhR §71).

However, this institution requires that human beings have acquired the ability to respect others and themselves as property holders and *act* accordingly – in particular, to restrain themselves in accordance with the property claims of others insofar as they are in line with institutional norms. In turn, this requires the ability for self-control discussed in connection with the "educational argument". If that ability has not yet been widely acquired in a group, there are no property rights that could protect members of that group against enslavement or other forms of forced labour, either. Hence, until forced labour has fulfilled its disciplining task in a group, it is qualifiedly justified also insofar as group members have not reached personhood, with the consequence that there is no rational basis for institutionalised property rights that could protect them: "Slaves are not persons, for they want according to their drives, needs, but not as a free subject".[176]

3. *Cowardly contract argument.* There is another element in the 1807 dialectic of lordship and bondage that Hegel later uses to supplement further his qualified justification of forced labour: the notion that the master–servant hierarchy emerges because one of the subjects has surrendered. This later becomes the basis for different versions of what has been called the "cowardly-contract" defence of slavery[177] – slavery and forced labour, more generally, are justified because the enslaved or servant could have chosen death instead: "[W]hen a human is a slave, it is their will; for they do not need it; they can kill themselves".[178] Moreover: "One who cannot risk their life for their freedom is worth being a slave".[179]

The first quote suggests that slavery is qualifiedly justified as the enslaved consented to their condition by preferring it over death. This is a weak argument even by the lights of a pro-slavery advocate, as it obliterates the difference between forced obedience and free consent. The second quote points to a somewhat different argument, which is further illuminated by a denigrating remark Hegel makes on African societies: "there is the greatest lack of consciousness of personality in this condition; this is why they let themselves enslave so easily".[180] Hegel assumes here a particular explanation for why the enslaved did not risk or actually take their own lives, an explanation that is directly connected to the status of personhood that we just discussed.[181] For Hegel, such personhood has a reflective dimension: it requires an *awareness* of oneself as a person who respects others and themselves as property holders and is able and willing to act accordingly – i.e., of oneself as possessing personal freedom.[182] Against this background, Hegel takes the fact that the enslaved are

---

[176] GW 26.2:617$^{18-21}$.   [177] Binder (1989: 1441).
[178] GW 26.2:822^{30}-823^{3}, cf. 26.1:361$^{10f.}$.   [179] GW 25.1:114^{5f}, cf. PhSG 3:69.
[180] GW 25.1:35$^{34-36}$; cf. PhH 153/GW 27.4:1226$^{13-18}$; GW 14.2:435$^{3f.}$.   [181] PhR §35.
[182] PhR §211.

still alive to show that they lack such awareness of freedom (otherwise, they would have risked and lost their lives to defend their liberty).[183] It follows that they also lack personhood and hence (per 'argument from personhood') protection by institutionalised property rights. (Notice that Hegel also endorses the flip side of this argument: the enslaved always have the right to escape.[184] When they do so, they demonstrate that they have acquired personhood and that their enslavement is no longer justified.)

To summarise the results of this subsection: Hegel thinks it follows from central elements in the dialectics of lordship and bondage and his mature social philosophy that forced labour is justified during stages of socio-cultural development where individuals are not yet enabled to self-control by ordinary processes of socialisation. At such stages, forced labour is justified, for Hegel, (1) as a necessary evil that, in virtue of its disciplining function, is required for the realisation of freedom (educational argument), and (2) insofar as members of such societies lack personhood, and hence also institutionalised property rights that would protect them against forced labour (argument from personhood); moreover, (3) such lack of personhood is proven by the fact that forced labourers have not preferred death instead (cowardly contract argument).

3.4 Justifying Transatlantic Slavery

That Hegel takes the arguments examined in the last subsection to apply to the specific case of transatlantic slavery becomes particularly clear in a passage from his lectures on the Philosophy of History in 1830/1831. In the context of a discussion that contrasts transatlantic slavery with domestic slavery in Africa (an issue we will return to shortly), he declares (in Karl Hegel's transcript): "Slavery is in and for itself unjust, for the essence of humans is freedom; but they first must become mature for it and while the Europeans acknowledge that slavery is indeed wrong, they would act equally unjustly if they would immediately bestow freedom upon the negro slaves".[185] Wichern's version adds: "the taming of their natural disposition has to precede their real freedom".[186] Here, Hegel explicitly ascribes the disciplining function that the educational argument hinges on to transatlantic slavery. As this entails that the enslaved Africans lack the self-control needed for personhood, the argument from personhood applies here, too, and it is clear from the passages we cited in connection with the 'cowardly contract argument' that Hegel takes this argument to apply to enslaved Africans, as well.

---

[183] By contrast, the 1807 version postulated a sudden "fear of death" as causing the surrender.
[184] GW 26.2:627$^{4-6}$; 26.3:1156$^{22-30}$.   [185] GW 27.4:1229$^{19-22}$, cf. PhH 157.
[186] GW 27.4:1230$^{22f.}$.

Hegel's view that people from sub-Saharan Africa lack the abilities required for self-control is part of his hierarchical metaphysics of race (cf. Section 1.4). Hegel claims that they are characterised by "unbridledness",[187] by "sensuous caprice with the energy, power of the sensuous will",[188] unable to develop a grasp of universal norms ("the universal does not raise in their heads")[189] or to subordinate their actions to a shared "universal purpose".[190] Lacking personhood and the awareness of one's personal freedom that comes with it, "man" in Africa "does not have genuine respect for himself and for others"; Africans fail to appreciate the "absolute value that humans have in themselves",[191] which purportedly leads to mutual enslavement.[192]

So, while in Asian and European societies, the necessary stage of forced labour belongs to a "prehistorical" past,[193] Hegel confabulates innate racial characteristics of Africans that, he claims, prevent them from developing abilities of self-control and corresponding practices of education – apparently, both insofar as said characteristics make it particularly difficult for Africans to learn to control themselves and insofar as they cause slave-holders within domestic African slavery to be capricious masters,[194] who further impede such learning and even, Hegel believes, cannibalise the enslaved.[195] For these reasons, Africans are stuck in "the intermediary condition between the state of nature and the transition to a more developed state",[196] i.e., in relations of mutual enslavement and arbitrary despotism, and "are not able themselves to overcome their naturalness".[197] This also means, for Hegel, that Africans have so far been unable to build more advanced socio-political institutions, in particular states[198] – hence Hegel's notorious claim that sub-Saharan Africa has never entered world history.[199]

For Hegel, people from Africa are therefore not protected by property rights against enslavement (per 'argument from personhood' and 'cowardly contract argument'), and they still need to undergo some form of forced labour further to eventually become able to participate in free societies (per 'educational argument'). But in addition, Hegel can use his racial assumptions about Africans also to argue that it is specifically *enslavement by a supposedly more advanced racial group* that is justified here as a 'necessary evil' rather than the relevant

---

[187] GW 27.4:1229^8, cf. PhH 157. [188] GW 27.2:522$^{17f.}$, cf. PhH 154. [189] GW 25.1:35$^{36f.}$.
[190] GW 25.1:234^{25}. [191] GW 27.2:520$^{26f.}$, cf. PhSG 2:53, 55, PhH 153.
[192] GW 27.2:521^{29}–522^5, cf. PhH 153. [193] GW 27.4:1236^{12}. [194] GW 27.2:521^{18}.
[195] GW 27.4:1229$^{37f.}$, cf. PhH 153. [196] GW 25.1:35$^{32f.}$, cf. PhH 154. [197] GW 25.1:36$^{4f.}$.
[198] RH 186/GW 27.2:522$^{27-32}$. – This contrasts with Pinkard (2017: 52f.), who holds that for Hegel, African societies are deficient 'only' insofar as they lack space for critical reflection on the given norms and institutions.
[199] E.g., PhH 157/GW 27.4:1230$^{6-8}$. Cf. Bernasconi (2000), Tibebu (2011); on the neocolonial legacy of this claim: Mbembe (2007); on the emergence of statehood as beginning of world history: LPhW 114/GW 18:190^8–191^{24}.

alternatives, namely (a) domestic African slavery and (b) a less brutal regime – like feudal servitude or the subsistence economy of the Jesuit reductions. As to (a), Hegel imagines enslavement by Europeans rather than Africans to be a "mode of becoming participant in a higher morality and the culture connected with it":[200] it ensures that the enslaved do not get cannibalised, it subjects them to a form of forced labour that is more orderly than in African domestic slavery, and it puts the enslaved in contact with European culture. In particular, it forces the enslaved to carry out agricultural labour, which, as we will see in Sections 4.4 and 5.3, has its own educating effect in Hegel's view.

Regarding (b), we saw already that Hegel refers to transatlantic slavery as a "taming of the natural disposition" of the enslaved.[201] The choice of the term "taming" – as if the slave-holders were trying to domesticate wild animals rather than mistreating fellow human beings – suggests the following reading: given the racial characteristics ("natural disposition") of Africans, only their brutal treatment in slavery, not some 'milder' form of forced labour, is apt to exert the required disciplining function that will eventually change the relevant racial characteristics (cf. Section 1.4). Notice that this reading is coherent with our findings in Section 2: Hegel sees European colonialism as racial domination; its precise modality should depend on the supposed racial characteristics of the colonised and enslaved.

To wrap things up: for Hegel, transatlantic slavery is justified up until the point when the enslaved have collectively become capable of self-control and participation in a norm-governed society; it is justified during that time both insofar as the enslaved lack protection by property rights, and because given the racial characteristics of Africans, enslavement by a racially superior group, in this case the Europeans, is required as disciplining means for them to become capable of self-control and, ultimately, freedom.

3.5 Hegel on Abolition

Having thus reconstructed the arguments by which Hegel purports to qualifiedly justify forced labour, and in particular the enslavement of Africans, we can now examine what position in the contemporary debate on abolition his views might align with.

Let us first consider the state of the British debate in the 1820s. After the campaign against the British slave trade eventually led to its ban in 1807, the focus of the debate moved initially to other European countries' slave-trading activities. By contrast, calls for the abolition of slavery itself became loud only in the 1820s, and even then (and until ca. 1830), the dominant view among white

---

[200] PhH 157/SW 12:129. [201] GW 27.4:1230^{22}.

abolitionists called for *gradual* rather than *immediate* emancipation.[202] It was thought that slavery had such a corrupting and dehumanising effect that the enslaved were not presently capable of living in freedom. Instead of immediate abolition of slavery, there was a need, in this view, for a transitional phase of mitigated captivity in which the enslaved would slowly get accustomed to freedom. (This contrasts with the immediatist positions championed by Black abolitionists – such as the 1823 Demerara insurgents whose demands Hegel could read about in the British newspapers – and by female white abolitionists, including Elizabeth Heyrick, author of the seminal 1824 pamphlet *Immediate, Not Gradual Abolition*.[203])

Importantly, the notion that slavery should be gradually abolished because the enslaved persons were not considered to be ready for freedom was also common, at least at the level of public rhetoric, among plantation lobbyists of that time. They realised that by espousing this position, they could maintain the status quo while pleasing public opinion. As historian Gordon Lewis observes, this "was merely a desperate effort to save time; emancipation was accepted, but always at some safe, distant future date, never at the present moment".[204] Hence, gradualism about emancipation was common ground between most British abolitionists and the plantation lobby in the 1810s and 1820s; the difference between the parties lay in the justifications they gave for the alleged need for continued slavery[205] and in the practical implications of those justifications. Rather than pointing to the disastrous psychic effects of enslavement as the abolitionists did, planters were more likely to argue for gradualism on racial grounds, claiming that Africans qua race are uncivilised and incapable of freedom[206] – and implying that slavery would, therefore, have to remain in existence much longer than abolitionists would think.

A further ambiguity of British debates on slavery of that time concerns the attitude towards the enslaved persons' liberation struggles. While some abolitionists welcomed and defended the slave uprisings,[207] the perception of the Haitian Revolution as a brutal massacre against the white population of Saint Domingue was widespread among the British public.[208] This led to the view, common also among white abolitionists, that "emancipation symbolised all the horrors of race war dramatised in St. Domingue".[209] Indeed, many white abolitionists distanced themselves from the violence of slave rebellions, emphasising that they demanded gradual reform of slavery, not its sudden overthrow.[210]

---

[202] Williams ([1944]2022: 173); Turley (1991: 29–38); Matthews (2006: 16f.).
[203] Midgley (1992: 101–116); Coleman (manuscript).
[204] Lewis (2000: 556); cf. Dumas (2016: 14).   [205] Dumas (2016: 43).   [206] Ibid. (47).
[207] Matthews (2006: 71 and passim).   [208] Ibid. (59–61, 145f.).   [209] Ibid. (146).
[210] Ibid. (35); Dumas (2016: 53).

Given this background in the 1820s, how did Hegel think about the abolition of slavery in that period? The available lecture transcripts relate two occasions on which Hegel takes an explicit stand. First, an anonymous transcript of the lectures on the Philosophy of Right in 1821/1822 reports the following statement "concerning the abolition of slavery": "As horrible consequences were feared from sudden abolition, one looked for slower means. The principle is right, but it belongs to a concrete state of affairs, which can demand more than that this relation gets suddenly severed. Slaves who have never been free, are in need of an education".[211]

The second statement is found in transcripts of the lectures on the Philosophy of History in 1830/1831; we have already quoted parts of it:

> Slavery is in and for itself unjust, for the essence of humans is freedom; but they first must become mature for it and while the Europeans acknowledge that slavery is indeed wrong, they would act equally unjustly if they would immediately bestow freedom upon the negro slaves: as the French did at the time of the French Revolution; the horrible consequences became immediately manifest; quite rightly, the Europeans proceed slowly < and gradually [*stufenweise*]> with the manumission of negroes <, the taming of their natural disposition [*Naturell*] has to precede their real freedom>.[212]

Besides, Wichern offers a more detailed version of the remark on "horrible consequences": "When it [sc. immediate emancipation] happens, things have been more dreadful than in the French Revolution, and the latter is insignificant, compared to the state of affairs that has there [sc. in Haiti] emerged out of it [i.e. immediate emancipation]".[213]

In both passages, Hegel contrasts the 'immediate' French abolition of slavery in 1793/1794 with the gradualist policies of other "Europeans". These passages directly relate to the British debate in the 1820s that we have outlined at the beginning of this subsection: (a) Hegel addresses in both passages the abolition of *slavery*, not of the slave trade; (b) he favours both times *gradual* over immediate abolition; (c) on the ground that currently enslaved persons are not *ready for freedom*; (d) as witnessed by the events after the French immediate emancipation in 1793/1794 (i.e., anti-planter violence during the *Haitian Revolution*).[214] As we

---

[211] GW 26.2:662$^{28-33}$.

[212] GW 27.4:1229^{18}–1230^2, Karl Hegel's version, parts in <> from Wichern's version: GW 27.4:1230$^{22f.}$; cf. PhH 157.

[213] GW 27.4:1229$^{42f.}$.

[214] Hegel was wavering in his views about the Haitian Revolution. Elsewhere, he takes it to show that the formerly enslaved have become capable of a life in freedom – even though he treats this as a beneficial result of European colonialism, thus downplaying the agency of the revolutionaries: "The formation of a Negro state in the West Indies is remarkable. So, the possibility of human freedom is also present in Africans, but they are not able themselves [*es liegt nicht in ihnen*] to overcome their naturalness" (GW 25.1:36$^{3-5}$). Cf. also GW 14.2:435$^{4-8}$, where he classifies slave rebellions as mere "conspiracies" that served particular rather than universal interests.

saw, points (a)–(c) were common tenets in both parties in that debate, and (d) was shared at least by some abolitionists with the planter lobbyists.

We also saw that what set apart the parties' arguments were their justifications for prolonging slavery, together with their practical implications. In this regard, Hegel's two passages differ significantly. In the first passage, he argues for the need for "education" for enslaved persons who have never been free. This is consistent with the abolitionist position that explains the alleged unreadiness for freedom by the adverse effects of enslavement on the individual. In the second passage, by contrast, Hegel postulates a "natural disposition" on the side of the enslaved Africans that stands in the way of freedom, thus squarely endorsing the planters' race-based version of gradualism.

While the exact coincidence with the arguments on (a)–(d) in the British debate makes it very likely that Hegel is echoing contemporary British sources here, he admittedly may not have been entirely clear about the dynamics of the debate in that period. Instead, his main point in this context may have been that the gradualism he could find across the British debate of the 1820s vindicated his position on slavery in PhR §57 Remark. Still, of Hegel's two statements on gradualism, only the one from the 1830/1831 lectures that aligns with plantationist gradualism really coheres with his overall position. Hegel's insistence on the purported 'disciplining' role of slavery (Section 3.4) presupposes an incapacity for freedom that precedes enslavement (as affirmed in the 1830/1831 passage), rather than being its effect (as the 1821/1822 passage appears to assume). We should therefore take the 1830/1831 statement as his considered position – with the troubling implication that, on this issue, he offers elaborate philosophical support to the position of the slaveholders.

***

Let us take stock. We have seen that transatlantic slavery plays a more prominent role in Hegel's mature thought than is often assumed. Drawing on Thomas Clarkson's 1786 *Essay on the Slavery and Commerce of the Human Species*, Hegel discusses it in detail in the *Philosophy Right* (§57 Remark), and conceptualises the issue of its legitimacy as an antinomy. Given his processual view of freedom and the dialectic of lordship and bondage, slavery is neither outright illegitimate nor outright legitimate for Hegel. Instead, he assigns it a place in the process that creates the preconditions for freedom. This means that forced labour is legitimate during a particular stage in that process – a position Hegel seeks to establish through extensive philosophical elaboration, including the 'educational argument', the 'argument from personhood', and the 'cowardly contract argument'. Moreover, in line with his view of European colonialism as racial domination and his racist theory of human diversity, Hegel deems transatlantic slavery – one of the most cruel atrocities in the history of humankind – a necessary and appropriate means for enabling African and Afrodiasporic people to live in freedom. Because of its race-based character, Hegel's resulting plea for the merely gradual abolition of slavery coincides with the most prominent position the enslavers took in the contemporary British debate – a finding that stands in stark contrast with the popular view of Hegel as a philosopher of freedom *par excellence*.

4 Hegel and British India

In his later years in Berlin, Hegel developed a keen interest in India. He spent much effort to keep himself updated on the emerging orientalist literature of his time; he lectured on Indian literature, religion, and philosophy; and he took Wilhelm von Humboldt's 1826 essay on the *Bhagavad Gita* as occasion for writing an extended review essay in which he also presents his own account of Indian society, Hindu religion, and Yoga philosophy. Yet while his discussions often also refer to contemporary Indian society and culture (which he thinks have remained basically unchanged since ancient times[215]), the extant texts contain only relatively few remarks on British rule in India. It is therefore not surprising that the rich secondary literature on Hegel and India has, to our knowledge, almost exclusively focused on his views about classical Indian literature, religion, and philosophy,[216] and not systematically addressed Hegel's remarks on British India so far. We hope to close this gap and show that those remarks, if seen in their historical context, allow us to reconstruct the outlines of an assessment of colonial India that provides an illuminating contrast to Hegel's treatment of the colonisation of the Americas and the enslavement of Africans.

4.1 Historical Context

Most of Hegel's extant writing and lecturing on India dates from between 1818 and 1831 and, therefore, coincides with a crucial juncture in the political and ideological history of British rule in India. In 1818, the British victory over the Maratha empire meant that, after the decline of the Mughal empire in the early eighteenth century and the military successes against the French and their Indian allies in the mid-eighteenth century, no serious contender was left to

---

[215] GW 27.2:572$^{13-15}$; 27.3:898$^{21f.}$.
[216] Cf., with further references, Rathore & Mohapatra (2017); see Guha (2003: 42f.) for an exception.

the dominion of the East India Company over the subcontinent. Until then, the Company had expanded and consolidated its power in India.[217] It violently looted the country and used intrigue and treachery to play off local rulers against each other.[218] But when it came to matters of custom and religion, the Company was pursuing, in this phase of consolidation, a relatively cautious attitude vis-à-vis the huge population in the newly gained territories.[219] Until 1813, when the British Crown granted it sovereignty over India, the Company was hostile to the activities of Christian missionaries in the country. It tried to base its administration of law and tax on the local traditions,[220] and even paraded troops in honour of Hindu deities.[221] Indeed, in the eyes of its most vocal domestic critic, Edmund Burke, it was a major flaw that the British made no attempts at 'modernising' the conquered Indian territories: "England has erected no churches, no hospitals, no palaces, no schools; England has built no bridges, made no high roads, cut no navigations, dug out no reservoirs".[222] How true this comment was to the policy of the East India Company is witnessed by the fact that decades later, the British official George FitzClarence (1794–1842) still felt the need to respond to Burke in his 1819 memoir, *Journal of a Route Across India, Through Egypt and to England*, one of Hegel's sources on India.[223] FitzClarence's reply is pragmatic: bridges "would have been carried away by the torrents in the rains", and roads and channels would have been useless "in a country where all travel by water in boats capable of comfort and shelter".[224] As to churches, company officials were prudent enough to realise that any attempt to intervene in religious matters – and hence also in everyday customs and ceremonies – would be perceived as a sacrilege and could trigger rebellion. As FitzClarence sums up the received Company doctrine: "I do not see any cause which at present exists in India ... to shake our government over this part of the world, that is to say, if we respect the prejudices of the natives [and] do not attempt to subvert their religion by the introduction of our own ... ".[225]

Such strategic caution was complemented by relatively sympathetic attitudes towards Indians and their cultural legacy, which were common among the British in India at this time.[226] Not only did Company members and administration officials socialise with Indians and sometimes even adopt Indian manners,[227] but several of them also began to engage in serious scholarship on ancient India. The translations of the *Bhagavad Gita* (translated by Charles Wilkins in 1785) and the play *Sakuntala* (translated by William Jones in 1789),

---

[217] Sharma (2017: 19f., 27).   [218] Ray (1998: 513f.).   [219] Ibid. (510).   [220] Cohn (1989).
[221] Sharma (2017: 50).   [222] Burke ([1783]1981: 402).
[223] BG 138/GW 16:73$^{33f.}$; 27.2:571^{32}–572^{1}; 27.2:581$^{5f.}$.   [224] FitzClarence (1819: 233).
[225] Ibid. (161); cf. Sharma (2017: 50f.).   [226] Varma (2010: 31–34); Sharma (2017: 49f.).
[227] Sharma (2017: 49–51).

as well as William Jones's discovery of the Indo-European language family, were initially met with enthusiasm – also in Germany, where authors like Herder, Schiller, Goethe, and in particular Friedrich Schlegel and Wilhelm von Humboldt joined Jones and others in their admiration for Indian culture.

Since the late eighteenth century, such positive attitudes, as well as the early Company policy in cultural and religious matters, were challenged by advocates of evangelisation. Pro-missionary politicians like Charles Grant and missionaries like William Ward and Jean-Antoine Dubois published writings in which the case for evangelisation was built on denigrating accounts of Indian society and culture. The caste system, the self-immolation of widows (*sati*), various 'superstitious' beliefs and ceremonies, and an alleged general moral depravation of native Indians were depicted at length as so many reasons that made it necessary to propagate Christianity in the country. This campaign proved very influential: not only did the parliament's Charter Act in 1813 allow Christian missionaries to India, but the missionary literature also had a significant impact on the way Company officials would perceive and rule the country in the period after 1818 when the East India Company had consolidated its power on the subcontinent.[228]

A pivotal place in this process belongs to James Mill's three-volume *History of British India* (1817). Building partly on the missionary accounts and their anti-Hindu fervour, partly on the conjectural histories of the Scottish Enlightenment with their theories of different stages of civilisation (more on this in Section 5), and partly on Benthamite utilitarianism, Mill offers a lengthy discussion of Hinduism, traditional Indian society, literature, culture, and "manners" that takes the defamation of everything Indian to new excesses.[229] Mill's declared goal in this discussion is to "ascertain the true state of the Hindus in the scale of civilisation" so that Britain could adequately "adapt ... " its government "to the state of the people for the use of which it is intended".[230] In explicit opposition to "admirers of Hindu civilisation"[231] like William Jones and his followers, he argues that after some early innovations, India had remained stuck in a "semi-barbarous"[232] stage of cultural development.[233] Mill uses hundreds of pages to detail alleged abuses and instances of "superstition"[234] in this "rude"[235] and "ignorant"[236] culture with its "loose, vague, wavering, obscure, and inconsistent" religion,[237] citing the same instances as the missionaries, adding others (like the oppression of women),[238] and denying or downplaying all qualities that India's "admirers" had found in the Sanskrit texts. In an appendix to his chapter on "Manners", Mill quotes a highly tendentious selection from statements that

---

[228] Cf. Sharma (2017: 50). [229] Pitts (2005: 123–133). [230] Mill (1817: 1:429).
[231] Ibid. (647). [232] Ibid. (405n.). [233] Ibid. (120). [234] Ibid. (106, 131).
[235] Ibid. (98 and passim). [236] Ibid. (106). [237] Ibid. (215). [238] Ibid. (293–302).

Hegel and Colonialism 37

British judges in India had supplied in response to an inquiry in 1801 about the impact of British administration on the "general moral character of the inhabitants",[239] as well as passages from anti-Hindu writers such as Grant, Dubois, and Ward.[240]

Mill is reluctant to make specific policy recommendations in his *History*. However, in subsequent years, when the book was required reading for those who entered a career in the East India Company,[241] it would feed the mills of so-called Anglicists who wanted to introduce English as the language of instruction, together with other reforms. This party rose to power with the appointment of William Bentinck as governor-general in 1828, who would, in the following years, carry out far-reaching reforms, including the abolition of *sati* (1829).[242] The new policy stood in stark contrast with the company's earlier approach. It was informed by attitudes of open racialised disdain towards Indians and their culture – attitudes which directly derive from the "psychology of contempt"[243] at work in the anti-Hindu writings of authors like Grant, Dubois, Ward, and Mill.

4.2 Hegel on India

Hegel's discussions of India should be read against the background of this changing conjuncture in British colonial discourse and policy. In his lectures on the History of Philosophy of 1818/1819, Hegel cites Dubois and Ward – two of the pro-missionary authors – as main sources[244] and follows their critique of India. In his 1822/1823 lectures on the Philosophy of History, subsequent lectures and the *Bhagavad Gita* essay, Hegel offers an expanded and even more denigrating account of India. As Leuze (1975: 80–88) has shown in detail, much of this account is directly adapted from Mill's *History*. Hegel follows Mill, Dubois, and Ward in their charges of superstition, irrationality, and despotism, in their catalogues of flawed institutions and customs,[245] and in their essentialising claims about vicious traits allegedly typical of Indians – in particular, their "ethical depravity":[246] "Deceit and cunning are the fundamental characteristics of the Indian. Cheating, stealing, robbing, murdering are with him habitual".[247] Hegel also explicitly refers to the reports of judges and missionaries cited by Mill, estimating them to be "[e]specially authentic testimonies".[248] To this, he adds not

---

[239] Ibid. (322). [240] Ibid. (323–325, 328–331). [241] Sharma (2017: 158). [242] Ibid. (35f.).
[243] Ibid. (29). [244] GW 30.1:29^1.
[245] The caste system: GW 27.3:899^{13}–902^{18}, cf. PhH 209–213; the oppression of women: LPhW 268f./GW 27.1:165^8–166^9; *sati*, female infanticide and other forms of religiously motivated self-mutilation and suicide: PhH 215f./GW 27.4:1281^{11}–1282^3.
[246] LPhW 271/GW 27.1:168^{16}.
[247] PhH 225/GW 27.4:1289$^{13\text{-}15}$, translation modified; cf. also LPhW 302/GW 27.1:204$^{2f.}$, 16:22$^{8f.}$.
[248] GW 27.3:910^6.

only further textual 'evidence' for denigrating characterisations – both from Sanskrit texts such as the law book of Manu and from contemporary scholarly publications – but also his own systematisation[249] in terms of a basic opposition between, on the one hand, a tendency to dissolve all content in an empty conception of the divine (his reading of Brahma) and, on the other hand, an unrestrained indulgence in sensuous phantasy.[250] Ultimately, these features are rooted in the character that Hegel ascribes to the "Mongolian" race, namely, an unresolved opposition between an indeterminate universality and a self-enclosed individuality[251] that entails an "eternal despotism".[252] By thus introducing the anti-Hindu position of authors like Ward and Mill into the German debate, Hegel attacks German orientalists like Friedrich Schlegel and Wilhelm von Humboldt, using the assessment of Indian culture as a proxy for other disagreements.[253]

Hegel's dismissal of ancient Indian cultures matches his partly uncritical, partly affirmative attitude towards British rule. This becomes evident when he touches upon issues which the Company's critics had addressed. Whereas Diderot blames the British for having failed to help the starving masses during the 1769/1770 famine,[254] Hegel describes at length the attempts of the British to codify the traditional revenue system,[255] which were at least a partial cause of the famine, but fails to mention the latter. Whereas Burke criticises the Company for its treacherous dealings with local rulers,[256] and Kant attacks it for its "incitement of the various Indian states to widespread wars",[257] Hegel acknowledges these intrigues and resulting wars but claims that in dealing politically with India, "only a relation to violence, subterfuge and deceit is possible, no treaty".[258] The notorious Warren Hastings, who had been put on trial for mismanagement and personal corruption and symbolised the ills of British rule in the eyes of its critics, is referred to by Hegel as the "great Governor General of India".[259]

All this could lead us to expect that besides general endorsement of British rule in India, Hegel also sympathises with calls for a more intrusive form of colonial regime. Interestingly, this is not what we find in his comments. Instead, in his 1824/1825 lectures, Hegel gives examples of how British militaries allowed Indian troops to observe their religious norms even where this created

---

[249] Cf. Rajan (1999: 105).   [250] GW 27.3:912^{24}–913^{7}; PhH 225/GW 27.4:1289$^{8-13}$.
[251] GW 25.1:235$^{1-7}$, cf. PhSG 2:57.   [252] GW 25.2:612^{6}, cf. LPhS 91.
[253] Cf. Rajan (1999: 241); Rathore & Mohapatra (2017: 19f.) – Hodgson's claim that Hegel's sources on India were "prejudiced" as they "reflected the attitudes of the British East India Company" (cited by Rajan, 1999: 241n., cf. also Pinkard, 2017: 53) is thus oversimplified. Different authors whom Hegel was familiar with took starkly contrasting attitudes, and Hegel made conscious decisions as to which of these assessments he would adopt.
[254] Muthu (2003: 88).   [255] LPhW 265f./GW 27.1:161^{11}–163^{7}.
[256] Burke ([1783]1981: 391).   [257] Kant (1902ff.: 8:358f.).   [258] GW 27.2:594$^{11f.}$
[259] BG 89/GW 16:21^{33}.

practical difficulties for the army, and comments: "the English distinguish themselves [*zeichnen sich dadurch aus*], and they hope to have success, by respecting the customs and peculiarities of peoples so highly".[260] He further expands on this point in 1826/1827: "The English respect the castes, tolerate calmly everything".[261] For one thing, this is prudent as it allows them to "maintain such a huge realm under their rule":[262] to illustrate this, Hegel refers to the 1760 siege of Pondicherry, where the French general Lally-Tollendal ordered Indian soldiers irrespectively of their castes to dig out trenches. This led to a mutiny, followed by a decisive French surrender to the British.[263] In addition, Hegel claims that the British approach of toleration also effects a gradual change in Indian customs: "Bit by bit, but not by violence, the English bring it about that the Indians abandon their allegiance to their strict rules. ... [T]he English treat them exactly as their laws demand. Through this indulgence, a lot gradually disappears by itself".[264] The transcripts allude to an example that does not get further explained: the use of cow leather in the uniforms of Indian soldiers.[265]

Hegel's point becomes more apparent if we look at his source – the 1819 travel journal by George FitzClarence cited in Section 4.1 for its rejoinder to Burke. FitzClarence not only advocates the established Company approach of religious and cultural toleration but also argues that this very approach has led to considerable social change in India.[266] His examples include the one to which Hegel alludes. Despite initial concerns about leather pieces possibly coming from sacred cows, Indian soldiers gradually adapted and finally completely took over the British uniforms: "The gradual change of dress", FitzClarence remarks, "has strongly marked the advance of our conquest over their prejudices".[267] FitzClarence is eager to emphasise that such change could only occur due to the respectful behaviour of British officials and soldiers and the "attachment" and "affection" that this engendered among the Indian troops.[268] The opposite effect results, FitzClarence argues, where colonisers attempt to impose a change in customs – as witnessed by the case of Lally-Tollendal (cited by Hegel, too) who, "with the besotted obstinacy of ignorance, attempted, abruptly and violently, to break through their habits".[269]

Hegel thus directly adopts FitzClarence's views and examples regarding the British strategy of toleration: it stabilises British rule, but it also leads Indians to assimilate to European customs – and should, therefore, be preferred to the more invasive approach that the missionaries were demanding.

---

[260] GW 27.2:580$^{26-28}$. [261] GW 27.3:907$^{8f.}$. [262] GW 27.3:907$^{9f.}$.
[263] GW 27.3:907$^{10-17}$. [264] GW 27.3:908$^{1-3, 6-8}$. [265] GW 27.3:908$^{3-6}$.
[266] FitzClarence (1819: 260). [267] Ibid. (260). [268] Ibid. (262f.). [269] Ibid. (265).

Hegel further elaborates on these points in the section of his lectures dedicated to Britain itself. There, he claims that members of modern British society are characterised (even qua "innate" traits)[270] by exclusive attention to "particular purposes",[271] i.e., their material interests as economic agents. According to Hegel, this leads to a "complete indifference towards the nationality of other peoples"; nor do they "make pretensions about their own".[272] As a result, Hegel believes, the British "calmly tolerate each superstition, all customs".[273] Comparison with the almost identical remarks we cited from Hegel's discussions of India suggests that he is referring here, first and foremost, to British rule in India. Hegel goes on to enthusiastically praise British colonial policy: "[The British] have in virtue of all these reasons the destiny [*Bestimmung*] of being missionaries of civilisation. They scrutinise [*durchspehen* [sic]] everything, arouse needs in the most remote countries – expand commerce [*Verkehr*] towards all sides of the Earth, and do the most to make barbarians human".[274]

By postulating a distinctively British mode of colonisation that is anchored in the British 'national spirit' with its focus on economic interests, characterised by toleration and an absence of chauvinism, and centred on the promotion of trade, Hegel connects the topic of British rule in India to the traditional ideological framework that contrasted British colonialism with the Spanish colonialism of 'conquest' (cf. Section 2). Like other contemporary observers,[275] Hegel seems to see British rule in India as the most modern version of the allegedly less brutal British approach to colonialism. This version is entirely focused on economic advantage rather than conquest and settlement. For him, this approach is also most efficient in civilising "barbarians", therefore bestowing on the British the providential role ("destiny") of "missionaries of civilisation" (a notion that we will explore in more detail in Section 5). Moreover, Hegel alludes here to a further possible explanation for the civilising effect of British toleration, besides the gradual assimilation due to relations of attachment and trust as FitzClarence describes it: the establishment of trade connections brings about new needs among the groups thus connected, thus triggering processes of social development that Hegel accounts for in his theory of civil society.[276]

This latter point shows that while Hegel's endorsement of the Company's strategy of toleration seems to have its direct inspiration in FitzClarence, it is also embedded in a broader systematic context in Hegel's thought. Besides the cultivating role of commerce, this context includes the notion of the 'national spirit' of a people – i.e., the geographically and racially conditioned basic

---

[270] GW 27.3:1141^9.   [271] GW 27.3:1141$^{3f.}$ [272] GW 27.3:1141$^{9-11}$.
[273] GW 27.3:1141^{11}.   [274] GW 27.3:1141$^{12-15}$, cf. PhH 567.
[275] Cf. Pagden (1995: 6f.) on Talleyrand.   [276] PhR §§190–198.

principle that underlies the various aspects of social and cultural life characteristic of a people.[277] As we will see in the following subsection, not only the 'national spirit' of the British colonisers but also that of the colonised Indians figures in Hegel's argument.

4.3 The Role of 'National Spirit'

In a passage from an 1822/1823 lecture on the Philosophy of Right, Hegel discusses the constitution that Napoleon gave to Spain in 1808, known as the Bayonne Constitution. Hegel points out that this attempt to impose a constitution "a priori" did not go well; the Spanish did not accept the new constitution: "[A] constitution is not something that is just made ad hoc, for a constitution is the work of centuries, the Idea, the consciousness of the rational, in so far as it has developed in a nation. And this consciousness cannot be made".[278] Even though the Bayonne Constitution was "more rational" than the previous organisation of the Spanish empire, the Spanish "rejected it as something alien because they were not yet educated to this point".[279]

Importantly, what Hegel finds wrong about the Bayonne Constitution is not that it was imposed from the outside and hence suffered from a deficit of political autonomy. Instead, Hegel makes a point here that he shared with authors like Montesquieu and Herder: a nation's political organisation needs to grow organically out of its history and to express the characteristics of its 'national spirit'. In particular, it needs to reflect the "consciousness" that defines this national spirit at a given stage of history, i.e., the collective understanding of freedom that has emerged in this society. Without such fit, the institutions of a state will be alienating for its citizens and thus undermine their freedom – even in a case as the Bayonne Constitution, in which those institutions formally allow for *more* freedom than what would correspond to the citizens' collective understanding of freedom. However, the passage also implies that the consciousness of freedom connected to a 'national spirit' at a given stage of history is not static. It can develop through further collective 'education', but this education needs to be incremental and organic.

Mutatis mutandis, the same reasoning can be applied to other aspects of social life that, in Hegel's view, express the 'national spirit' of a people and its corresponding way of collectively understanding freedom. This includes "its religion, its political institutions, its ethical life, its system of justice, its customs, as well as ... its science, art, and technical skill, and the direction of its

---

[277] Cf. Enc. §394; PhR §§340, 346f.; LPhW 118/GW 18:196^{24}–197^{4}.
[278] GW 26.2:1011$^{27-30}$; cf. LNP 239–241/GW 26.1:163^{6}–165^{6}; LPhR 198f./GW 26.1:530^{6}–531^{5}; 26.3:1425$^{7-20}$.
[279] GW 26.2:1012$^{4f.}$.

industry".[280] In these cases, too, the imposition of foreign ways of life will lead to alienation, and modernisation can come about only through slow, gradual change.

It is not difficult to see how such considerations were relevant to Hegel's views on India and could provide a deeper systematic reason for his sympathies with FitzClarence's argument. Unlike Napoleon in Spain, the British in India leave, at least in Hegel's understanding, the country's institutions mostly intact: they merely take over governmental control and encash the revenues; they attempt to build legal and tax administration on existing traditions and steer clear of interventions in such dimensions as religion and customs. Given Hegel's views about 'national spirits', it was very natural for him to assume that such a policy favours processes of gradual cultural and social modernisation and, ultimately, changes in the collective understanding of freedom, i.e., the 'national spirit' of Indians, that would enable them in the long run to live in a modern, non-despotic state[281] – a result that bestows world-historical legitimation on British colonialism, as we will see in Section 5. The same underlying views would lead him to expect that the alternative approach of deep intervention proposed by the missionaries would cause alienation and unrest and impede rather than promote change.

4.4 Contrasting India with America and Africa

How could Hegel endorse the Company's non-interference in local customs, arguing that it would favour social and cultural modernisation, when he also claims that, in the case of people of African and American origin, there was a need for such extreme forms of domination as transatlantic slavery and the Jesuit reductions? Would consistency not require him to either demand a more invasive colonial regime also for India or to hold that something like the model of cautious assimilation described by FitzClarence ought to replace slavery in the Americas?

We can answer this question by examining Hegel's views about Asia's specific racial and geographic conditions more closely. Hegel characterises the Asian or "Mongolian" race, of which the 'national spirit' of India is a specific modification, as an opposition between universality and individuality (as we saw in Section 4.2). This characterisation entails for him that the mental and social abilities supposedly characteristic of that race go beyond the immersion into nature which he imagines obtaining in Africa and America. While Africans exist, according to Hegel's racial phantasies, in "pure natural unity and desire",[282] and Americans "live entirely for the moment, like animals",[283] he

---

[280] LPhW 118/GW 18:196^{26}–197^{2}. [281] Cf. PhR §347 Rem.
[282] GW 25.2:611^{14}, cf. LPhS 91. [283] PhSG 2:65/GW 25.1:23^{29}.

thinks that in the mental life of Asians, universality emerges as a distinct element. Because of their race-specific mental abilities, they can grasp and construct universal contents like Manu's laws or the conception of the divine as Brahma.[284] For Hegel, this also means that they can go on their own through the processes of individual and social learning that, in his view, make subjects capable of self-control, personhood, and participation in norm-governed systems of mutual recognition such as law and property (cf. Section 3).

Hegel thinks that the geographic circumstances of Asia match such racial characteristics.[285] While sub-Saharan Africa primarily consists of infertile high plateaus that only support nomadic life, and the "immature" geography of America, with its swamp lands and massive streams, leaves little room for human culture,[286] the large Asian river plains, with their fertile mud, offer ideal conditions for agriculture.[287] As we will see in more detail in Section 5, Hegel considers agriculture a decisive step in developing human culture. Commenting on the Asian river valleys, he points out: "Agriculture intrinsically includes fixedness, ceasing of wandering, it achieves provision for the future, and as reflection enters here and one provides for the family in a general manner, the principle of property and craft is present in it".[288]

Hegel points here to three important features of agriculture. First, unlike the nomadic form of life to which (Hegel thinks) pre-colonial societies in America and sub-Saharan Africa were and are bound, agriculture requires settlements where families claim property over the land they cultivate and its fruits. To be able to manage conflicts between such claims, farmers need to establish a system of private property that requires mutual recognition as persons with property rights – i.e., the kind of personhood that presupposes, as we saw in Section 3, learning processes such as the dialectic of lordship and bondage. Second, farmers must store a part of the harvest, both as a reserve for the cold season and as seed for the next seed time. Hence, they have to exercise precisely the kind of self-control that the bondsman learns towards the end of Hegel's dialectic of lordship and bondage. Third, since agriculture requires such economic planning ("reflection") as well as agricultural tools, it prepares the ground for a craft economy and, hence, for urbanisation – which in turn creates a need for more comprehensive and centralised forms of social order, including government and legal administration.

Hence, Hegel thinks that in pre-colonial Asia, the necessary racial and geographic preconditions for private property, law, and statehood were in

---

[284] GW 25.2:612^{3f}, cf. LPHS 91.
[285] In James & Knappik (2023: 116), we argue that Hegel sees geography and race as two corresponding ways in which the characteristics of continents get manifested.
[286] LPhW 195/GW 27.1:83$^{1-5}$. [287] LPhW 199/GW 27.1:87$^{5-8}$. [288] GW 27.2:528$^{26-29}$.

place, unlike in Africa and pre-colonial America.[289] There is, therefore, no further need here for the educational processes that – in Hegel's view – justify the colonial oppression of Africans and Indigenous Americans. The same considerations also explain why, for Hegel, the views about 'national spirits' that underpin his critique of the Bayonne constitution do not (presently) apply to Americans and Africans: for Hegel, pre-colonial American and African societies have been unable to develop a consciousness of freedom; hence, they lack a 'national spirit' in the sense of a shared "consciousness of the rational, in so far as it has developed in a nation".[290] Consequently, Hegel's assessment of British rule in India is yet another instance of Hegel's insistence on the character of colonial rule as racial domination that we have encountered in Sections 2 and 3.

5 The "Absolute Right" to Colonise

After examining Hegel's discussions of various manifestations of colonialism in the past sections, we now turn to the question of what normative framework Hegel builds upon in his various discussions of colonial phenomena. This question is particularly pressing in the case of India, as a region that has developed a legal order and statehood – preconditions for property and sovereignty rights that are, as we saw, absent for Hegel in the case of Africans and Indigenous Americans. However, addressing Hegel's normative framework will also deepen our understanding of why the 'educational' effects he claims for colonialism and slavery in the Americas provide qualified justifications for those forms of domination.

5.1 World History and "Absolute Right"

The normative framework of Hegel's views on colonialism is rooted in his central conception of history as a movement towards an ultimate goal – the complete realisation of the 'Idea', viz. the underlying principle of reality, through the unfolding of 'spirit', its principal manifestation, into full freedom. "This movement [of history] is the path of liberation for the spiritual substance, the deed by which the absolute final aim of the world is realised in the world".[291] More concretely, this "path of liberation" consists of both a gradually improving collective understanding of freedom and its realisation in corresponding social

---

[289] Hegel sometimes denies that India has brought about a state in the full sense of an organic whole (e.g., LPhW 282/GW 27.1:181$^{2-5}$, 27.4:1272$^{3f.}$; cf. Guha, 2003: 9). But elsewhere, he interprets the caste system as early form of functional articulation that prepares organic statehood (LPhW 258/GW 27.1:152^{3}–153^{5}), and recognises the existence of law (e.g., LPhW 265/GW 27.1:161$^{5-9}$) and private landed property (GW 27.2:580$^{1-3}$) in traditional Indian societies.

[290] GW 26.2:1011$^{28f.}$; cf. Bernasconi (2000: 187f.), quoting Enc. §394 Add., PhSG 2:69/SW 10:65.

[291] Enc. §549.

institutions.²⁹² Since this process realises the "absolute final aim of the world" – the goal around which finite reality as a whole is organised – at the 'worldly' level of political institutions ("in the world"),²⁹³ it has an overriding normative status: "This liberation of spirit, in which it proceeds to come to itself and to actualise its truth, and the task of this liberation, is the supreme and absolute right".²⁹⁴

The notion of such an "absolute right" of spirit (or "of the Idea")²⁹⁵ is a recurrent topic in Hegel's discussions of world history. Before examining how it relates to Hegel's assessment of colonialism, we must ask how he understands it more generally.

First, Hegel often uses the term 'absolute right' in grammatical constructions – such as with an infinitive clause, as in PhR §347 – that suggest he understands 'right' here in the sense of an entitlement to something, rather than as an uncountable noun denoting a normative order ("system of right").²⁹⁶ Nevertheless, there is a connection with the latter sense, too. For like right in the uncountable-noun-sense, the 'absolute right' gets administered (both *cognised* and *actualised*)²⁹⁷ by a court of law (*Gericht*): famously, Hegel describes world history (*Weltgeschichte*) as a court of law that passes judgment over the whole world (*Weltgericht*). Thus, world history judges (cognises) what the absolute right demands and actualises this right. It thereby achieves justice: "No people ever suffered wrong; what it suffered, it had merited".²⁹⁸

Second, by qualifying this right as "absolute" (or "highest"²⁹⁹), Hegel implies that it overrides other normative dimensions in his account of ethical life.³⁰⁰ These dimensions include abstract right, moral norms, and the norms of ethical life – such as those governing family life, professional ethics, and citizens' duties towards the state – as well as norms of international law: (a) the right of societies with a sufficiently organised "constitution" and "condition" to be recognised as sovereign states by other states;³⁰¹ (b) the norm that nations ought to maintain their treaties;³⁰² and (c) the norm that nations must first pursue their own good.³⁰³ Thus, Hegel states that against the "absolute

---

²⁹² LPhW 87f./GW 18:151³–153²².   ²⁹³ Cf. Enc. §552; PhR §360.   ²⁹⁴ Enc. §550.
²⁹⁵ Cf. LNP 306/GW 26.1:217²⁹; LNP 308/GW 26.1:219¹⁶; LPhW 175/GW 27.1:58¹⁶; GW 27.2:503⁷; GW 27.4:1199¹⁵; PhR §§340, 345, 347; "absolute right of the Idea": PhR §350. Cf. Wood (1990: 228) on how this notion follows from basic elements in Hegel's views about history and freedom.
²⁹⁶ PhR §4.   ²⁹⁷ PhR §219.   ²⁹⁸ LNP 307/GW 26.1:218²⁴ᶠ.   ²⁹⁹ PhR §340.
³⁰⁰ It remains connected to them insofar as its purpose is to advance the implementation of social orders with norms of these kinds.
³⁰¹ PhR §331.   ³⁰² PhR §333.
³⁰³ PhR §336. Cf. Wood (1990: 228f.). – As far as we can see, Hegel does not ascribe a separate dimension of normative assessment to the spheres of "absolute" spirit, i.e., art, religion and philosophy. These spheres are organically connected to socio-political history (LPhW 101f./

right", nations that do not 'carry the torch' of "the world spirit's development" are "without rights [*rechtlos*]";[304] sovereignty rights are "void" against it, and also "pity [i.e., morality], ethical life, and everything that in other spheres is sacred to [spirit]"[305] are trumped by the absolute right.

Third, the "absolute right" is "a right to which no state can appeal <against another state>".[306] This does not mean that individual humans cannot meaningfully grasp or discuss that absolute right. But the appropriate place for such discourse is the philosophical interpretation of history: an interpretation that brackets evaluations in terms of moral and ethical norms[307] and of international law[308] to grasp how justice is done to the absolute right of spirit in history – to offer a theodicy in world history.[309]

Some de- and postcolonial scholars have rightly stressed that Hegel's notion of an "absolute right" provides an ideal basis for the justification of colonialism.[310] However, as far as we can see, no closer analysis has been provided yet of how exactly Hegel's statements on the "absolute right" bear, from the viewpoint of his system, on the issue of colonialism.[311] It is the task of the following subsections to offer such an analysis.

5.2 *Philosophy of Right* §§349 and 350: The "Right of Heroes to Establish States"

In the *Philosophy of Right*, Hegel identifies world history with the "development of the state to constitutional monarchy".[312] This "development" is a teleological process in which each of the "moments" of the state – its constitutional powers and the forms of government they embody – are first each one-sidedly articulated as distinct forms of government, in which one, few, and many rule.[313] In modernity, these different forms of government are then incorporated as the constitutional powers of the modern state, where "concrete freedom"[314] is first fully realised. Thus, actualising the "final aim of the world" involves the development of full-blown statehood, the nature of which Hegel accounts for in his 'organicist' theory of the state.[315] There, Hegel characterises

---

GW 18:172^{19}–173^{19}); advancements in them ultimately consist in improved conceptions of freedom, which rightfully demand political realisation – as in the case of religious wars, e.g., between Catholics and Protestants in Early Modern Europe (PhH 541–546/GW 24.7:1550^{20}–1554^{16}).

[304] PhR §347, cf. Enc. §550. [305] LNP 306/GW 26.1:218$^{12,\ 16f.}$, translation modified.
[306] RH 124/GW 27.2:498^{1}. Translation modified, part in <> from transcript Dove, GW 27.2:498^{31}.
[307] PhR §345. [308] RH 124/GW 27.2:498$^{18f.}$; cf. Wood (1990: 229).
[309] LPhW 85/GW 18:150^{6}.
[310] Dussel (1995: 24f.); Rajan (1999: 113); cf. Pradella (2014: 443).
[311] Existing discussions tend to focus on the question whether the absolute right exempts world-historical individuals from moral norms: Wood (1990: 228–236); McCarney (2012: 113–119).
[312] PhR §273. [313] PhR §273 Rem. [314] PhR §260. [315] PhR §§257–329.

the "political constitution" of the modern state in terms of a structure he calls its "self-determination":[316] a process in which the state maintains itself through differentiating its "moments", i.e., constitutional powers or organs that mutually constrain and thereby maintain each other's activity such that they each robustly contribute to legislating, deciding, and executing what the state wills.[317] The full development of this structure is what actualises freedom and, thus, the end of world-historical development.[318] Therefore, it also serves as the standard against which degrees of political organisation are assessed in the court of law of world history.

Against the background of this theory, Hegel discusses a first aspect of the "absolute right of the Idea"[319] that directly bears on colonialism in §§349f. In §350, Hegel specifies that this is a right of the Idea "to make its appearance in legal determinations and objective institutions, beginning with marriage and agriculture". Regarding the latter two institutions, Hegel references the Remark to §203, where he connected them to the emergence of states. Similarly, the preceding section had described the "transition of a family, tribe, kinship group, mass [of people], etc. to the condition of a state" as the "*formal* realisation of the Idea"[320] – "formal" because what matters to this transition is the institutional form of organisation that societies acquire, in particular the rule of law.[321]

Hegel makes two crucial claims regarding this transition. First, prior to it, societies have no sovereignty.[322] Hence, societies that have not developed states with legal orders – as is the case, in Hegel's view,[323] with pre-colonial societies in Africa and the Americas – have no sovereignty rights that they could appeal to against invading colonisers. But second, the account in §350 also adds a positive claim: it is part of the "absolute right" that the institutions necessary for statehood be created. Hegel further explains that this entails a "*right of heroes* to establish states", even where this "may appear ... " "as violence and wrong [*Unrecht*]".[324] Since the term "hero" in this context primarily refers to foundation myths of ancient Greek city-states,[325] it could seem that this passage has little to do with European colonialism. But for one thing, acts that can appear as "violence and wrong" are justified for Hegel in such cases because they achieve the transition from prestate to state order and thus are supported by the "absolute right". The same reasoning applies to colonialism and transatlantic slavery: due to their alleged 'educational' role, they ultimately enable Africans and Indigenous Americans to live in states.

---

[316] PhR §272. [317] PhR §§257f., 269–272, 275–279; cf. James (2020). [318] PhR §360.
[319] PhR §350. [320] PhR §349. [321] Ibid.; LPhW 179/GW 27.1:64[1f.]. [322] PhR §349.
[323] GW 25.1:35[32–34]; LPhS 91/GW 25.2:611[7, 28f.], 27.2:518[6]. [324] PhR §350.
[325] Cf. LPhA 252/GW 13:291f.

For another, the examples Hegel seems to have in mind here are closer to European colonialism than one may first suspect. As lecture transcripts suggest, Hegel was thinking in particular of figures who, according to mythology, had founded states by introducing agriculture and marriage – the two central factors for the transition towards statehood according to §§350 and 203 Rem.: "The founders of states were chiefly the heroes who introduced marriage and agriculture".[326] Hegel is drawing here on his friend Georg Friedrich Creuzer's *Symbolik und Mythologie der alten Völker, besonders der Griechen* (1810–1812), which he explicitly cites in PhR §203 Rem. Creuzer observes that ancient mythologies commonly ascribed the introduction of both agriculture and marriage to the same heroes (*Heroen*).[327] In particular, in the case of Cecrops,[328] the mythical founder and first king of Athens, Creuzer cites accounts that describe him as an Egyptian who led a group of colonisers from Sais[329] – for Creuzer an instance in support of his view that migration and cultural influences from the Orient were crucial to the rise of Greek culture.

Not only does Hegel endorse this view in general,[330] he also cites Cecrops to illustrate that archaic Greece was ruled by kings whose families were originally Asian and North African settlers.[331] Hence, when Hegel talks about the "right of heroes to establish states" in PhR §350, the "heroes" are not necessarily autochthonous lawgivers – they can also be colonisers who teach the local population the achievements of their culture, including statehood and its cultural preconditions. PhR §350 thus provides a first specification of the "absolute right" that can be seen as legitimising modern European colonialism, too.

5.3 *Philosophy of Right* §351: 'Civilisation' and Four-Stages Theories of Social Development

In PhR §351, Hegel further expands on the implications of the "absolute right of the Idea" by focusing on the topic of different degrees of 'civilisation'. Compared to the argument in §350, he introduces two new aspects. First, he broadens the scope to also include, besides marriage and agriculture, hunting, pastoralism, "etc." – we will come back to this presently. Second, he shifts perspective. While he previously discussed the "absolute right" from the vantage point of his philosophical account of world history, he now addresses a perspective located within history. Particular historical agents – namely, "civilised nations" – consider "less advanced" peoples as "barbarians" that are legitimate targets of conquest: they act in the "consciousness that the rights

---

[326] LPhR 243/GW 26.1:583$^{3-5}$. [327] Creuzer (1810–1812: 2:402f., cf. 2:460).
[328] Ibid. (1:364, 2:401f.). [329] Ibid. (1:265, cf. 2:146, 400f.)
[330] LPhW 374/GW 27.1:287$^{8-10}$; LPhW 376/GW 27.1:290$^{10f.}$.
[331] LPhW 376/GW 27.1:291^{3}.

of these other nations are not equal to theirs" and they "regard and treat their [i.e., the other nations'] independence as something merely formal".[332] As Hegel explains before, to regard the independence of a nation as "merely formal" means not recognising its sovereignty.[333] Hegel refers here to ancient Greek attitudes towards 'barbarians',[334] but not only. As Anthony Pagden has shown, the discourse of civilisational superiority and a corresponding right of conquest creates a continuity between the ancient Roman ambition to civilise the whole world,[335] the Christian goal of converting humankind to Christianity,[336] and colonial discourse from the sixteenth to the nineteenth centuries.[337] In other places, Hegel cites instances of this ideology from various periods, including evangelisation as justification for Columbus's conquests in America[338] and the technical view, prominent in the natural law tradition,[339] that the life of 'uncivilised' peoples is an offence to humankind that requires violent intervention ("[p]edagogical coercion, or coercion directed against savagery and barbarism"[340]) – for example, through colonial conquest.

While Hegel does not directly address in this section whether actions motivated by such ideology are justified, he does imply that the atitude as such can be based on the "absolute right of the Idea" (cf. the beginning of §351: "From the same determination, it happens that ... "). The *subjective* attitude in question is itself well-founded because the rights of the less civilised groups, including their "independence", are *objectively* trumped by the "absolute right" represented by the more 'civilised' nations.[341]

But how precisely is 'civilisation' relevant to the "absolute right of the Idea"? And does the argument in this section cover only cases where conquest, in Hegel's view, establishes statehood in the first place – as in the Americas – or does it also include instances where more 'civilised' nations conquer existing states, as in British India?

To address these questions, it will be helpful to consider more closely the examples that Hegel provides for degrees of civilisation: hunting, husbandry, and agriculture. As readers in his time would have known, these terms echo a central strand in later eighteenth and early nineteenth-centuries social thought: various authors, especially in France and Scotland, tried to use contemporary reports about non-European cultures, and in particular about Indigenous American societies, as basis not only for classifying different forms of social organisation (as did Montesquieu) but also for developing hypothetical reconstructions of the remote past of European societies (e.g., Rousseau).[342] Among thinkers of the Scottish

---

[332] PhR §351, translation modified. [333] PhR §349. [334] GW 27.1:308^7, cf. LPhW 390.
[335] Pagden (1995: 20, 23). [336] Ibid. (29). [337] Ibid. (126, 198f.).
[338] PhH 515/GW 27.4:1530$^{14f.}$. [339] Pagden (1995: 61). [340] PhR §93 Rem.
[341] Cf. PhR §347. [342] Meek (1976: 76–91).

Enlightenment, this approach was most fully elaborated into what became known as the four-stages theories of social development. As Ronald Meek has argued in his classical study on this topic,[343] Scottish thinkers like Adam Smith, Adam Ferguson, John Millar, and James Steuart postulated that changes in the mode of subsistence drove social development and that there was a series of four stages, defined by their dominant modes of subsistence, that every society could in principle go through: (1) hunting and gathering (members of such societies were often called "savages", following Montesquieu);[344] (2) nomadic husbandry ("barbarians" in Montesquieu's terminology)[345]; (3) sedentary agriculture; (4) commerce. Stages 1 and 2 were seen as exemplified by Indigenous societies in America, stage 3 by Egypt and some Asian societies,[346] and stage 4 by modern and some ancient European societies. The development of social institutions was thought to correspond closely to this sequence of stages. Thus, it was common to place the emergence of systems of law and government in the agricultural stage.[347] Millar followed Locke in locating the introduction of private property in the agricultural stage,[348] while Ferguson thought that there was private property, e.g., in herds and pastures, already in the nomadic stage.[349] In Ferguson's view, the same holds for servitude,[350] while for James Steuart, servitude resulted from the establishment of an agricultural society.[351]

The modes of subsistence that Hegel mentions as examples in PhR §351 exactly match the first three stages of the Scottish authors:

> From the same determination, it happens that civilised nations regard and treat as barbarians other nations which are less advanced than they are in the substantial moments of the state (as with *pastoralists* in relation to *hunters*, and *agriculturalists* in relation to both of these, etc.) ... (emphasis added, translation modified).

It is no coincidence that the sequence of stages cited here directly corresponds to Scottish theories. Hegel had closely studied key works of the Scottish Enlightenment in Bern and Jena,[352] and elements of four-stages theories are echoed in various contexts of his philosophy. Already in his treatments of the dialectics of recognition in Jena, Hegel can be seen as exploring how the transition from a state of nature to a state of right via the introduction of master–servant relations and private property is connected to husbandry and agriculture. Thus, in the 1807 *Phenomenology of Spirit*, the fact that the slave cultivates nature around himself is central to the slave's learning process.[353]

---

[343] Meek (1976). [344] Montesquieu ([1748]1995: XVIII.11; 1:536). [345] Ibid.
[346] Meek (1976: 66). [347] Millar ([1779]2006: 84f.). [348] Ibid.
[349] Ferguson ([1767]1996: 81). [350] Ibid. [351] Steuart (1767: 1:22). [352] Waszek (1988).
[353] PhS ¶195.

(Recall also Hegel's comments on agriculture cited in Section 4.4: agriculture requires provision for the future, and hence a form of self-control that servants learn through forced labour, according to the 1807 version of the master–servant dialectic; and cf. the versions in earlier Jena texts.[354])

That Hegel continues to engage with Scottish four-stages theories in his later thought becomes clear not only from PhR §351 but also when he connects at various places the four forms of subsistence to the characteristics of continents and races and the way world history is geographically located. Like many eighteenth-century authors, he claims that contemporary "North American savages" live in a "state of nature"[355] that lacks pastoralism and agriculture; the same holds for most people in the pre-colonial Americas in general.[356] This is due to the lack of cultivable grass plants[357] and suitable soil,[358] but also the racial characteristics that Hegel ascribes to Indigenous Americans, including their alleged inability to care for the future, which makes them also incapable of agriculture (cf. Sections 2.3 and 4.4). Besides, Hegel also cites another stock example of hunters and gatherers, derived from Tacitus, namely the ancient Germanic tribes in their "forests".[359]

By contrast, the infertile high plateaus and savannahs of Central Asia, sub-Saharan Africa and South America are inhabited by humans who typically live from nomadic pastoralism.[360] Again, this is partly due to geographic conditions not allowing for agriculture, and partly due to alleged racial characteristics: nomadic pastoralists, he points out, "are careless and provide nothing for the winter",[361] a feature that makes this form of subsistence available to those racial groups who, in Hegel's phantasy, (still) lack abilities of self-control and management for the future. Societies of this type are mainly organised around family ties and lack legal relations.[362]

A major break occurs between, on the one hand, these first two forms of society – which Hegel variously refers to as "state of nature",[363] "naturalness",[364] and "savagery"[365] – and, on the other hand, "civilised" or "advanced" (*gebildet*)[366] forms of social organisation, beginning with the agricultural societies that emerge in the floodplains and stream valleys of Asia and Egypt.[367] The fertility of these areas, but also the relatively superior mental characteristics that Hegel ascribes to Asians (and African–Asians, in the case of Egyptians),[368] enable these peoples to use a mode of subsistence which requires

---

[354] SEL 108f./GW 5:286^{13}–287^{29}; HHS 110/GW 8:214$^{1-7}$.   [355] GW 26.3:1309$^{32f.}$.
[356] LPhS 90/GW 25.2:610$^{9-11}$.   [357] GW 25.2:610^{14}–611^{1}.   [358] LPhW 195/GW 27.1:83$^{1-5}$.
[359] PhH 440/GW 27.4:1454^{16}.   [360] PhH 145/GW 27.4:1217$^{7-20}$.
[361] PhH 145/GW 27.4:1217$^{18f.}$.   [362] PhH 145/GW 27.4:1217$^{21f.}$.   [363] PhR §93 Rem.
[364] Ibid.   [365] LPhW 102/GW 18:174$^{18f.}$.   [366] LPhW 115/GW 18:191^{22}.
[367] PhH 146/GW 27.4:1218$^{12-18}$.   [368] Bernasconi (2007: 209).

a sedentary life, self-control, planning, and management, the use of methods (incl. awareness of natural cycles) and tools, as well as the division of cultivable land among different individuals and families.[369] As a result, private property, legal orders, and states have become both possible and necessary: "landed property and legal relations [*Rechtsverhältnisse*] begin, government and the states flourish in such countries".[370] Hence, Hegel's version of a four-stages theory only partially overlaps with his periodisation of world history in the *Philosophy of Right*, which takes the existence of states – and, thus, "civilised" forms of social organisation – as its starting point.[371] There, the agricultural societies of Asia correspond to the "Oriental Realm" and the commercial societies of ancient and modern Europe to the "Greek", "Roman", and "Germanic" realms.[372] Conversely, the hunter/gatherer and nomadic societies Hegel takes to pervade Central Asia, sub-Saharan Africa, and the Americas are not part of world history.

Against this background, Hegel's account of the dialectic of lordship and bondage with its references to agriculture can be seen as an attempt to explain how crucial elements of statehood – including relations of mutual recognition, norm-following, personhood, and subordination under a ruler or government – become available in the agricultural stage of social development. Agriculture, Hegel points out, is a "condition" that "brings with it the relation of lord and serf";[373] at the same time, "the combat of recognition and the subjugation under a master is the *appearance* in which man's social life, the beginning of states, emerged".[374] At this point, the justified violence addressed in PhR §350 can take the form of wars and domination among different families and clans.[375] Building on the 1807 dialectic of lordship and bondage, Hegel repeatedly emphasises how such phenomena have an educating role as they enable one to "work ... oneself free from the particular will and natural desires" and to create a "habit of directing oneself to an other", features that prepare the ground for a state whose citizens need to be capable of "knowing a universal and affirming its purpose".[376] (It is not a coincidence that this resembles Hegel's views on the educational role of slavery, cf. Section 3. Against the background of Hegel's engagement with the Scottish four-stages theories, we can now see how transatlantic slavery, in Hegel's understanding, 'enables' racial groups stuck in the stages of hunting/gathering and nomadism to proceed to the stage

---

[369] LPhW 202/GW 27.1:91$^{9-14}$; PhH 146/GW 27.4:1218$^{19f.}$.
[370] GW 27.4:1218$^{22f.}$, cf. LPhH 203/GW 27.1:91$^{33-36}$.
[371] PhR §340; LPhW 114/GW 18:190f. [372] PhR §355–358.
[373] PhH 525/GW 27.4:1536$^{15f.}$.
[374] Enc. §433 Rem.; cf. GW 25.2:789$^{1f.}$, LPhS 189, PhR §349 Rem.
[375] LPhS 190/GW 25.2:789$^{4-6}$. [376] LPhW 180/GW 27.1:65$^{5-8}$.

of agriculture – the enslaved were primarily forced to carry out agricultural work. By undergoing the same processes of education that had initially led to the emergence of states, the enslaved would – after generations – themselves become able to live freely in a state.)

Finally, the stage of commerce of the Scottish authors coincides with Hegel's civil society. Due to their alleged racial characteristics – in particular, the "audacity" of their "understanding"[377] – coastal societies in Europe have made persistent use of the opportunities that their geographic position offered for commercial exchange and related cultural and economic development – in contrast with cultures in Asia and North Africa, which refrained from shipping and maritime trade.[378] Through the mechanisms that Hegel details in his theory of civil society, trade connections supported processes of psychological refinement and social differentiation. In combination with what Hegel takes to be the characteristics of the Caucasian race (integration of individuality with "the true, substantial"[379]) and the Germanic 'national spirits' ('*Gemüth*' as a sense of totality[380]), such processes led to the emergence of a 'concrete' understanding of freedom, where individualisation goes hand in hand with participation in an increasingly 'organic' social whole.[381] Besides, the resulting familiarity with other cultures was one factor next to others (in particular, Christianity) that enabled Europeans to grasp freedom as belonging to *all* humans.[382] Taken together, these features made possible the emergence of the modern state – which contrasts with the 'despotism' of Asian states.

As this overview shows, the four modes of subsistence distinguished by the Scottish thinkers play a significant structuring role in Hegel's views on social development. This does not make Hegel a historical materialist; as part of "culture", i.e., how the "means for the satisfaction" of human "needs" are obtained in interaction with nature,[383] modes of subsistence belong to the "aspect of outer appearance and life" of societies, not to their "ideal aspect" of institutional organisation that is more directly pertinent to world history.[384] Nevertheless, Hegel remarks that "[i]n the history of states, occupations of people are important";[385] their modes of subsistence constrain and trigger processes of mental and social development that make possible social institutions in the first place.

This answers the first of our two questions, which asked why issues of 'civilisation' and modes of subsistence were relevant to the "absolute right" of the Idea: advancement in the mode of subsistence is a necessary precondition

---

[377] LPhW 205/GW 27.1:95^2. [378] LPhW 204/GW 27.1:93^{16}–95^3.
[379] LPhS 91/GW 25.2:612^{14}. [380] PhH 444/GW 27.4:1460$^{8-15}$; PhH 526/GW 27.4:1537$^{19f.}$.
[381] PhR §260. [382] LPhR 176/GW 26.1:502$^{18-23}$. [383] LPhW 190/GW 27.1:75^{24}-76^1.
[384] LPhW 189/GW 27.1:74$^{17f.}$. [385] LPhS 90/GW 25.2:610$^{37f.}$.

for advancement in the social realisation of freedom. Therefore, the absolute right of the Idea to "make its appearance in legal determinations and objective institutions"[386] entails a right for world history to replace less advanced by more advanced modes of subsistence, where this can occur through conquest of a less advanced by a more advanced group.

Our second question asked what cases of colonisation are covered by Hegel's argument. That Hegel directly refers to four-stages theories in this section should make it clear that in his enumeration – "pastoralists in relation to hunters, and agriculturalists in relation to both of these, etc." – the "etc." [*u.s.f.*][387] stands for the fourth stage, i.e., commerce or civil society, and its relationship towards the first three stages. Hence, the argument covers all cases where ancient and modern European societies (belonging to the fourth stage) colonise societies located at any of the first three stage. In particular, this includes Indigenous American societies (hunters), African societies (pastoralists), and Asian societies (agriculturalists).[388] In all these cases, the geographic and racial conditions of non-European societies 'fetter' them (to use a famous Marxist metaphor) in less advanced forms of subsistence and institutional life – in the case of India, in a "static" (*statarisch*)[389] agricultural society that does not advance to maritime trade and therefore does not on its own go beyond its 'despotic' understanding of freedom. In this logic, only foreign conquest and rule by a more 'civilised' nation can bring about the requisite social change.[390] Such interventions are therefore legitimised, qua means for the further social realisation of freedom, by the "absolute right of the Idea" which trumps the sovereignty of non-European states.

5.4 Two Objections

The interpretation of Hegel's argument in PhR §351 that we have presented in the last subsection can seem to stand in tension with some other passages in the Hegelian corpus. We discuss two principal objections in this subsection; this will also further clarify our reading.

First, in a discussion of religious wars in 1824/1825, Hegel claims that while "one of the parties involved will invariably claim to be defending a sacred principle in relation to which the rights of other nations are secondary and of lesser validity . . ., such situations can only arise where a proper state of right has not yet come into place".[391] Mark Alznauer takes Hegel to argue here that the

---

[386] PhR §350.   [387] Nisbet unfortunately omits this word from his translation.
[388] By contrast, the original four-stages theorists in the Scottish Enlightenment opposed the notion of later stages being superior: Pitts (2005: 26f., 37–40).
[389] GW 27.3:898^{20}.   [390] Cf. also PhR §347 Rem., LPhR 242/GW 26.1:581$^{3-7}$.
[391] RH 124/GW 27.2:498$^{8f., 13f.}$, translation modified.

"absolute right" only justifies events that establish states, not actions committed against existing states[392] – a view that would directly contradict our argument.

However, the passage in question can be understood in a way that is consistent with our interpretation of the "absolute right". In the same context, Hegel explains what he means by "proper state of right" (*eigentlicher Rechtszustand*) by identifying it with a "situation in which states enjoy true independence in their reciprocal relations";[393] i.e., a condition where they form part of a system of states that mutually recognise each other's sovereignty.[394] Given this clarification, Hegel's point may simply be the following: in such a context – e.g., in Europe after the Congress of Vienna[395] – it is not feasible for one state to start a war on another by appeal to an alleged higher religious right, e.g., of Protestantism over Catholicism or vice versa. The belligerent state would thereby undermine its own sovereign existence, as "the independence of each [state] is only respected in so far as the independence of the others is also recognised".[396] This point is fully consistent with our interpretation.

Second, there are passages suggesting that a "consciousness" of superiority towards other groups is itself something that needs to be overcome in the course of modernity. Thus, Hegel points out that the fact that ancient Greeks and Romans looked down upon others as "barbarians" reflects their limited conception of freedom.[397] Similar chauvinistic attitudes among modern European trading nations who thought that other peoples were "something worse than them" are condemned by Hegel as "narrow-mindedness" (*Borniertheit*), while the English are praised for having "started from the thought of the human", and thereby made the "whole world ... connected".[398] Quite generally, Hegel considers it an important positive effect of trade and commerce – hence, of the fourth stage of subsistence – that commercial nations become open-minded towards other cultures: trade requires mutual recognition as property owners.[399] Thus, "coming to know each other" enables people of different nations to "come out of their narrow-minded ideas".[400] This applies even to colour-based racism: "With this outlook arises the thought that someone can be a human being without behaving as we do, or without having the colour we do".[401]

Not only do these passages (a) seem to stand in stark contrast with Hegel's own denigrating comments about other peoples and races, but they also can (b) appear to undermine the notion that the "absolute right" of the Idea justifies a disregard for the rights of other groups that legitimises colonial conquest.

---

[392] Alznauer (2015: 182).   [393] RH 124/GW 27.2:498$^{15f.}$.   [394] PhR §331.
[395] Cf. LFA 2:1062/SW 15:353.   [396] RH 124/GW 27.2:498$^{2-4}$.
[397] LPhW 390/GW 27.1:308^7.   [398] LPhR 177f./GW 26.1:504$^{3-5}$, translation modified.
[399] LPhR 176/GW 26.1:502$^{33-35}$.   [400] LPhR 176/GW 26.1:502$^{23-25}$.
[401] LPhR 176f./GW 26.1:502$^{37f.}$.

Regarding (a), we have already argued in a parallel case in Section 2.2 that Hegel may be distinguishing (albeit rather artificially) between chauvinistic sentiments and what he took to be anthropological theory. Indeed, his hierarchical theory of race does not deny that the members of the different races are all human and, therefore, all share the intrinsic value that comes with this.[402]

Concerning (b), Hegel knew very well that the East Indian Company with its policy of conquest, intrigues, betrayals, and plunder showed little respect for Indians as sovereign citizens, property owners, or trade partners. The open-mindedness for which he praises the British colonisers is therefore best understood as restricted to their cultural and religious toleration,[403] an attitude which does not exclude disregard for Indigenous property and sovereignty rights per PhR §351.

6 Conclusion: Hegel and His Legacy

6.1 Hegel's Position in the History of Pro-Colonial Thought

In the preceding sections, we have found that for Hegel, the overall purpose of realising freedom in history vindicates European colonialism. As we saw, what precise form of colonial regime is appropriate in each case depends on the supposed racial characteristics of the colonised/enslaved: in the case of African and Indigenous American people, massively invasive forms of colonial rule like slavery and missionary paternalism are required to teach the mental preconditions for institutions such as agriculture, private property, legal systems, and states. For Indians – and presumably, Asians in general, given that he attributes them with comparatively 'advanced' racial characteristics and anticipates further European expansion in Asia, cf. Section 1.3 – Hegel suggests a different approach. This approach involves tolerating existing institutions and customs, promoting gradual cultural assimilation, and ultimately advancing the colonised in their understanding of freedom.

Given that we find this account of colonialism in his work, what position does Hegel occupy in the history of colonial discourse? On the one hand, his stance on colonialism is reactionary in many respects. His justification of colonialism echoes arguments from 'civilisation' that had been used throughout the centuries to legitimise conquest;[404] his notion of historical world realms reappropriates eschatological interpretations of world history, including colonialism, from earlier centuries;[405] his insistence on an 'educating' function of enslavement restates a position that was common in the seventeenth century.[406] If Sankar Muthu is correct in observing that "[t]he latter half of the eighteenth century is

---
[402] E.g., GW 25.1:33³⁷-34⁵; PhSG 2:47/GW 25.1:236¹³⁻¹⁵; cf. James & Knappik (2023: 109, 116).
[403] GW 27.3:1141⁹⁻¹¹. [404] Pagden (1995: e.g., 20, 100). [405] Ibid. (42f.). [406] Ibid. (99).

an anomalous period in modern European political thought, for it is only then that a group of significant [white] thinkers" – such as Diderot, Kant, Herder and Burke – "attacked the very foundations of imperialism",[407] Hegel must be counted as one important figure who contributed to shutting down this intellectual space of early white philosophical anti-colonialism.

Yet precisely because of this, Hegel's position is also uncannily prescient in many respects. His hierarchical theory of race, his transformation of Scottish four-stages theories into a tool of colonial legitimisation, his dismissal of contemporary enthusiasm about non-European cultures, his denial of Indigenous statehood and sovereignty, and his reclaim of a civilising function of colonisation are elements that anticipate much later nineteenth-century colonial practice and theory.[408] In the German context, Hegel is one of the first authors to present "systematic" colonisation as remedy for crises of overproduction and overpopulation – ideas that would soon become pivotal for those arguing in favour of German colonies.[409] What sets Hegel apart from the dominant nineteenth-century 'liberal imperialism' is, first and foremost, his view that the colonisers of Asia should not try to change the colonised actively. By contrast, authors like Alexis de Tocqueville, John Stuart Mill, and Friedrich List would quite generally see an active policy of education and assimilation as an important task of colonial rule, a 'burden' that Europeans must consciously take upon themselves, rather than leaving it to world history and the cunning of reason to complete that mission.

6.2 Hegel's Pro-Colonial Legacy

Hegel's racialised, Eurocentric conception of the history of political institutions, art, religion, and philosophy, which partly belittles, partly denies the achievements of non-European groups in these areas,[410] has had a lasting impact on 'coloniality', the conceptual and cultural framework of European colonialism that remains in vigour long after the former European colonies have reached formal independence.[411] This is evidenced, for example, by the continued Eurocentricity of the philosophical canon, which is arguably to an important extent due to Hegel's influence.[412]

Hegel's more specific theoretical engagement with colonialism has been consequential, too. For instance, his defence of slavery was cited by a Southern delegate, the slaveholder and fierce supporter of slavery, Lucius Quintus Cincinnatus Lamar, during US Congress debates on slavery in 1860.[413]

---

[407] Muthu (2003: 259).   [408] Lindley (1926: 18f.); Pitts (2005).   [409] Fenske (1991).
[410] Tibebu (2011); Guha (2003); Mbembe (2007); Park (2013); Stone (2020).
[411] E.g., Maldonado-Torres (2007: 244f.).   [412] Park (2013).   [413] Hoffheimer (1993).

It was also adopted by several of the St Louis Hegelians, who stood on the side of the Union in the Civil War but argued that there had been a necessary role to play for slavery up until then.[414] In particular, William Torrey Harris, one of the St Louis Hegelians and US Commissioner of Education from 1889 till 1906, used a thoroughly Hegelian account of racial hierarchy, historical progress, and education towards freedom as the basis for elaborating and implementing the US program of off-reservation 'American Indian boarding schools'. In this program, children of Indigenous Americans were forced to abandon their families, cultures, and languages and to undergo a Western education, often leading to physical and mental illness, death, and suicide.[415] Indigenous boarding school programs are nowadays recognised and investigated as grave historical injustices that form part of the colonial history of countries like the USA. This is, therefore, a case where the pro-colonial and racist elements of Hegel's thought not only left a mark on subsequent debates but also concretely shaped an instance of colonial oppression.

Hegel's philosophy has left its marks on pro-colonial discourse in other parts of the world, too. Thus, the aggressive imperialism of Heinrich von Treitschke, staunch supporter of Bismarck's colonial policy from 1884 onwards, has been linked to Hegel's views on nations' world-historical significance.[416] But also the view found in Marx and many of his followers that European colonialism, despite its character of brutal domination, is a necessary modernising force can be connected to the Hegelian legacy in Marxist conceptions of history.[417] Egid (2024) argues that discourse on Italian colonialism under fascism is shaped by Hegelianism; Murthy (2024) shows that the Pan-Asian thought of Japanese scholar Okakura Tenshin (1863–1913) draws on Hegel's notion of ethical life to argue for the superiority of traditional Asian compared to modern European societies, but also argues for Japanese hegemony within Asia by using racial notions that are close to Hegelian terminology.

A particular thorough influence of Hegel's philosophy on subsequent pro-colonial thought is found in Great Britain, where the heyday of British Idealism, then the dominant philosophical movement in the country, coincided with the height of the British Empire in the late nineteenth and early twentieth centuries. On the one hand, authors like Edward Caird, Henry Jones, and J.H. Muirhead followed the founder of the movement, T.H. Green, in arguing that wars were always wrong and could not be justified by considerations such as a civilising mission.[418] In addition, they were critical of much of colonial history, including the contemporary Boer wars in South Africa, as driven by greed and involving

---

[414] Jaarte (2024).   [415] Beisecker & Ervin (2024).   [416] Megay (1958).
[417] Cf. Said ([1978]2019: 153–156); for discussion and further literature, Paquette (2012).
[418] Boucher (1994: 686).

brutal exploitation.[419] Yet such reservations did not keep them from endorsing colonialism (in their terminology, 'imperialism') as such. According to Muirhead, how colonies were acquired is irrelevant to whether their current possession by the metropole is justified.[420] Regarding this latter question, he and other British idealists emphatically favoured colonialism. Like others in the later nineteenth century, they argued that colonial rule is not merely legitimate (as Hegel thought) but a *duty* that 'advanced' countries like England have vis-à-vis their colonies. What sets the British idealists apart from liberal positions (such as John Stuart Mill's) is that they conceptualised that duty in specifically Hegelian terms.

This is particularly salient in several speeches that Edward Caird gave between 1883 and 1907 as master of Balliol College, a stronghold of Hegelianism. Caird is unambiguous in his support for "the imperial glory of England" and "the glory of raising barbarous races to civilisation and Christianity".[421] He offers two reasons. First, in a discussion of the concept of a nation, he presents a version of Hegel's theory of 'national spirits' and argues on that basis – like Hegel, cf. Section 4.2 – that England's "national idea",[422] its "distinct national consciousness",[423] involves a civilising "mission".[424] England's geographic situation and social advances made it natural for it to turn to "the life of naval enterprise".[425] As a result, he holds,

> We have become the great colonising nation, and the nation that has shown the greatest power of gaining the mastery over uncivilised races. And if our dealings with these races have too often been initiated in greed and violence, yet undoubtedly these have in the long run given place to an effort, such as perhaps hardly any other nation has made, to make our government tend to the good of the governed, and to open to the governed all the privileges of their governors. In this way, commerce with us has generally gone hand in hand with civilisation.[426]

Consequently, Caird suggests, England has "a special part to play in the great work of civilisation"[427] – echoing Hegel's view that each national spirit is assigned a particular task in world history and, specifically, the task of some to be "bearer of the present developmental stage of world spirit".[428]

The second reason Caird offers in favour of the British Empire is inspired by Hegel's organicist view of ethical life – the view in which genuine freedom requires an institutionalised form of communal life that is differentiated into various functional parts.[429] Since Caird, like other British idealists, adopted Green's cosmopolitan view of international relations (as opposed to Hegel's

---

[419] E.g., Muirhead ([1900]1997: 245). [420] Ibid. (245f.). [421] Caird (1907: 254).
[422] Ibid. (101). [423] Ibid. (112). [424] Ibid. (102). [425] Ibid. (113). [426] Ibid. (114).
[427] Ibid. (112). [428] PhR §347. [429] James (2020).

realism),[430] it was natural for him to expand the notion of organic unity beyond the nation-state to humankind as such:

> [H]umanity is no longer conceived by us as a mere aggregate of individuals, but rather as a growing social unity, a family of nations which, in spite of their differences and oppositions, are very gradually, but still certainly, being drawn together, and made into the members of one organism, a world community, in which each has a special function to discharge.[431]

Importantly, the organicist notion of such functional differentiation allows Caird and other British idealists[432] to reconcile cosmopolitanism with colonial hierarchies. Echoing the ancient notion of *Pax Romana*, Caird credits British imperialism with the "glory of extending the empire of peace and justice" – his characterisation of the ideal cosmopolitan unity[433] – "among men".[434] The British Empire is thus seen as a step towards an encompassing organic (and hence, hierarchical) international unity.

British idealist support for colonialism came to an abrupt end with World War I. The idealists saw Germany's imperialist policy as a key factor behind the war and turned to a wholesale rejection of imperialism in favour of an internationalist conception of equal human rights.[435] However, their earlier organicist view of international unity had left its mark on debates that eventually led to the foundation of the League of Nations (1920). Influential participants in those debates, such as the members of the Round Table Movement and South African scholar and Apartheid politician Jan Christiaan Smuts (who coined the term 'holism' for his version of an organicist worldview), had been steeped in British idealist thought during their studies in Oxford and Cambridge.[436] Following the idealists' pre-war views, they argued for a unity of nations compatible with hierarchical differences: the Round Tablers opted for an 'organic' community,[437] and Smuts directly suggested modelling the League of Nations on the British Empire.[438] The advice was heeded: the League of Nations deliberately maintained colonial hierarchies, for example, by assigning mandate status to former colonies that were not deemed ready for self-government.[439]

6.3 Hegel's Anti-Colonial Legacy

By far the most positive thing that can be said about Hegel in connection with colonialism is that his philosophy also was a major source of inspiration for a number of anti-colonial, anti-slavery and anti-racist thinkers, mostly coming

---

[430] Boucher (1994: 688). [431] Caird (1907: 61). [432] Cf. Kaymaz (2019: 1241f.).
[433] Caird (1907: 251) [434] Ibid. (254). [435] Kaymaz (2019).
[436] Morefield (2014: 103, 173, 180). [437] Ibid. (105).
[438] Morefield (2014: 172f.); Getachew (2019: 49). [439] Getachew (2019: 49–51).

from formerly colonised/enslaved groups.[440] Central to this aspect of Hegel's legacy is the dialectic of lordship and bondage. It has been used by historians as a tool for critical interpretations of slavery,[441] but also as a resource for philosophical interpretations of slavery and colonialism. Thus, in a chapter of *Black Skin, White Masks* that has attracted much scholarly attention,[442] Frantz Fanon draws on Hegel's 1807 text to analyse the colonial situation in terms of an absent struggle for recognition.[443] Another instance is found in Angela Davis's 1969 *Lectures on Liberation*. In the context of a philosophical reading of Frederick Douglass's first autobiography, she endorses Hegel's processual understanding of freedom[444] and uses the dialectic of lordship and bondage to analyse Douglass's liberation: by openly challenging the slave-breaker Covey, Douglass took advantage of the fact that the hierarchy between enslaver and enslaved person consists in relations of recognition that can be revoked.[445] Davis thus develops a neo-Hegelian account of liberation, which offers an alternative to Hegel's cynical view that forced labour itself has a liberating impact on the enslaved.

Moreover, Davis also taps an unused potential of Hegel's dialectic of lordship and bondage when she highlights how precarious the dialectical situation of the master is. While the 1807 version of the dialectic had problematised that position, as the master fails to obtain the recognition he was seeking and gets caught in a wanton-like situation of mere consumption, Hegel nowhere used this point to address the condition of slave-holders in his later discussions of transatlantic slavery (even though contemporary accounts described the "planter way of life" as "at once crassly materialist and spiritually empty"[446]). Fanon, too, offers a corrective on this point: it follows from his appropriation of the dialectic of lordship and bondage that when the coloniser denies recognition to the colonised, this has a dehumanising effect on the coloniser himself[447] – a point that was also made by others who drew on Hegel in theorising colonial oppression.[448]

We conclude our study by turning to a further anti-colonial heir of Hegel, the Trinidadian historian and philosopher C.L.R. James (1901–1989), who is of particular interest as he engages with the philosophy of history that underlies Hegel's pro-colonial views. In a 1971 series of lectures on his classical account of the Haitian Revolution in *The Black Jacobins* (1938), James explains that

---

[440] Kuch (2013); Mascat (2014); Renault (2021); Harris (manuscript). In James & Knappik (forthcoming), we examine how such appropriations became possible through a highly selective and creative engagement with Hegel's texts that undermined their pro-colonial potential.
[441] Patterson (1982); Davis (1999). [442] For a recent overview, cf. Hogan (2023).
[443] Fanon ([1952]2021: 216–222), cf. James & Knappik (forthcoming). [444] Davis (1971: 7).
[445] Ibid. (22f.); cf. Renault (2021); James & Knappik (forthcoming). [446] Lewis (2000: 550).
[447] Fanon ([1952]2021: 217). [448] Freire ([1970]2017: 44–49).

what first enabled him to see in that revolution the unactualised potential for the liberation of the entire African continent was Hegel's "speculative thought" – understood as thinking about current events as a stage in a goal-directed process,[449] here the emergence of "the African ... as an independent force in history".[450] In James's view, this process begins with the Haitian Revolution.

In his first published engagement with Hegel, *Notes on Dialectics*,[451] James accounts for the history of the labour movement through a reading of Hegel's *Science of Logic*. Crucially, James shifts focus from the traditional concept of the 'vanguard party' to ordinary people – the 'masses' – as primary agents of change, drawing on Hegel's logical concepts of 'movement' and 'essence' to transcend the reified categories hindering the international labour movement.[452] Across transient manifestations, like the 1848 revolutions, the First International and the Commune, the movement's 'essence' persisted, with international labour organisations incorporating past organisational experiences. James captures the overall movement of world history in three general claims: first, contradiction and its resolution in revolutionary 'leaps' is what propels world-historical development; second, such leaps are brought about by the autonomous movement of the masses; third, world-historical development is directed at universal freedom.[453]

In his 1971 lectures, James draws on this interpretation of Hegelian dialectics to restate the outlines of his earlier account of the Haitian Revolution. Indeed, many of the themes James explicates in his later work are already implicitly present in *Black Jacobins* – including the dialectic of organisation versus spontaneous action, as well as between leadership and mass action.[454] In 1938, James described his book as an account of "[t]he transformation of slaves, trembling in hundreds before a single white man, into a people able to organise themselves and defeat the most powerful European nations of their day" and, as such, "one of the great epics of revolutionary struggle and achievement".[455] In the Hegelian terms of *Notes on Dialectics*, this amounts to a 'leap' towards universal freedom brought about by the *self*-movement of the enslaved masses, resolving the 'contradiction' between the ideals of the French Revolution and the reality of enslavement at the hands of the French in Saint Domingue.

Unlike Hegel (cf. footnote 214), James does not see the Haitian Revolution as the result of a one-sided diffusion of European values in the colonies. Instead, as he elaborates in his work on the 'negro question' in the USA, emancipatory struggles in both the 'centre' and the 'periphery' are interconnected.[456] In particular, he views the struggle of African Americans as part of a transnational,

---

[449] James (2000: 72); cf. James ([1948]1980: 9); Ilieva (2024). [450] James (2000: 72).
[451] James ([1948]1980). [452] Ilieva (2024). [453] Ilieva (2024: 146). [454] Ilieva (2024).
[455] James ([1938]1989: ix). [456] Renault (2016).

transatlantic history of pan-African revolts. For James, the Haitian Revolution was thus a world-historical event in its own right that bears just as much on the European world as the French Revolution. Universalising the Enlightenment ideal of freedom that most European revolutionaries had, until then, restricted to Europeans, the revolutionary leap propelled Haiti *ahead* of Europe, "into the very forefront of the movement of the day".[457]

Although it still operates within Hegel's teleological framework of world history, James's alternative to the Eurocentric narrative that underpins Hegel's justification of colonialism offers a model for engaging with Hegel's legacy today. By confronting that narrative with the perspective of the colonised and the enslaved, Black radical thinkers like James and Davis lay the groundwork for new historical narratives – narratives that both accommodate the often-overlooked entanglement of Enlightenment thought with anti-colonial and anti-racist struggles (paradigmatically exemplified by the Haitian Revolution), and reframe these struggles as central to a philosophical conception of modernity. As foundation of a Black Enlightenment,[458] these struggles – and the philosophical ideas born from them – serve, in Charles Mills's image, as a "prism"[459] through which we can illuminate blind spots while revealing the untapped potential of central ideas in modern European philosophy. Not least because thinkers such as Davis and James are rarely discussed as philosophers, the project they initiated remains unfinished. As Paul Gilroy notes, "after the Hegelian and Marxist imaginings of figures like W.E.B. Du Bois and C.L.R. James" – and, we would add, Angela Davis – "the idea that the slaves' pursuit of human freedom could retain any broader philosophical ... importance was seldom considered seriously."[460] It is up to us today to build upon the foundations they have laid.

---

[457] Cited by Renault (2016: 42).   [458] Mills (2013).   [459] Ibid. (32).
[460] Gilroy (2011: 5). On W.E.B. Du Bois's possible engagement with Hegel, cf. Shaw (2013).

References

Works by Hegel

We reference Hegel's works and translations of them using the following abbreviations. Where section (§) or paragraph (¶) numbers are available, we cite those.

BG = (2017). On the Episode of the Mahabharata Known by the Name *Bhagavad-Gita* by Wilhelm von Humboldt. In Rathore and Mohapatra (87–139).

Enc. = (1992). *Enzyklopädie der philosophischen Wissenschaften im Grundrisse (1830)*. GW 20. (Translation for part 3, *Die Philosophie des Geistes*, §377–577: 2007. *Philosophy of Mind*, trans. W. Wallace, A. V. Miller & M. Inwood, Oxford: Oxford University Press).

GW = (1968ff.). *Gesammelte Werke*, ed. Nordrhein-Westfälische Akademie der Wissenschaften und Künste, Hamburg: Meiner. (References to GW contain volume, subvolume (where applicable), page and line number. E.g. GW $25.1:25^3$ = GW volume 25, subvolume 1, page 25, line 3).

HHS = (1983). *Hegel and the Human Spirit. A Translation of the Jena Lectures on the Philosophy of Spirit (1805–6) with Commentary*, trans. L. Rauch, Detroit: Wayne State University Press.

LFA = (1975). *Aesthetics: Lectures on Fine Art*, trans. T. M. Knox, Oxford: Clarendon.

LNP = (1995). *Lectures on Natural Right and Political Science: The First Philosophy of Right. Heidelberg 1817–1818 with Additions from the Lectures of 1818–1819*, trans. J. M. Stewart & P. Hodgson, Berkeley: University of California Press.

LPhA = (2014). *Lectures on the Philosophy of Art: The Hotho Transcript of the 1823 Berlin Lectures*, trans. R. Brown, Oxford: Clarendon.

LPhR = (2023). *Lectures on the Philosophy of Right, 1819–1820*, trans. A. Brudner, Toronto: University of Toronto Press.

LPhS = (2007). *Lectures on the Philosophy of Spirit 1827–8*, trans. R. Williams, Oxford: Oxford University Press.

LPhW = (2011). *Lectures on the Philosophy of World History. Volume 1: Manuscripts of the Introduction and the Lectures of 1822–3*, trans. R. Brown & P. Hodgson, Oxford: Clarendon.

PhG = (2005). *Die Philosophie der Geschichte. Vorlesungsmitschrift Heimann (Winter 1830/1831)*, ed. K. Vieweg, München: Wilhelm Fink.

PhH = ([1857]1901). *Philosophy of History*, trans. J. Sibree, New York: Collier. archive.org/details/friedrich-hegel/.

PhR = (1991). *Elements of the Philosophy of Right*, ed. A. Wood, trans. H. B. Nisbet, Cambridge: Cambridge University Press.

PhS = (2018). *Phenomenology of Spirit*, trans. T. Pinkard, Cambridge: Cambridge University Press.

PhSG = (1978). *Hegels Philosophie des subjektiven Geistes/Hegel's Philosophy of Subjective Spirit*, trans. M. J. Petry, 3 Vols., Dordrecht: Reidel.

RH = (1975). *Lectures on the Philosophy of World History. Introduction. Reason in History*, trans. H. B. Nisbet, Cambridge: Cambridge University Press.

SEL = (1979). *Hegel's System of Ethical Life and First Philosophy of Spirit*, trans. T. M. Knox & H. S. Harris, Albany: State University of New York Press.

SL = (2010). *Science of Logic*, trans. G. di Giovanni, Cambridge: Cambridge University Press.

SW = (1986). *Werke in 20 Bänden*, ed. E. Moldenhauer & K. M. Michel, Frankfurt: Suhrkamp.

Other Works Cited

Alznauer, M. (2015). *Hegel's Theory of Responsibility*, Cambridge: Cambridge University Press.

Andrade, É. (2017). A opacidade do iluminismo: O racismo na filosofia moderna. *Kriterion*, 137, 291–309.

Anonymous. (1810). Preussen, nach seiner Wiedergeburt. *Minerva*, 13(4), 449–472.

Beisecker, D. & Ervin, J. (2024). American Hegelianism and Its Impact upon Indian Boarding School Policy. *Hegel Bulletin*, 45(1), 65–92.

Bernasconi, R. (2000). With What Must the Philosophy of World History Begin? On the Racial Basis of Hegel's Eurocentrism. *Nineteenth-Century Contexts*, 22(2), 171–201.

Bernasconi, R. (2007). The Return of Africa: Hegel and the Question of the Racial Identity of the Egyptians. In P. Grier, ed., *Identity and Difference: Studies in Hegel's Logic, Philosophy of Spirit, and Politics*. Albany: State University of New York Press, 201–216.

Binder, G. (1989). Mastery, Slavery, and Emancipation. *Cardozo Law Review*, 10, 1435–1480.

Boucher, D. (1994). British Idealism, the State, and International Relations. *Journal of the History of Ideas*, 55(4), 671–694.

Bourke, R. (2023). *Hegel's World Revolutions*, Princeton: Princeton University Press.

Brennan, T. (2014). *Borrowed Light: Vico, Hegel, and the Colonies*, Stanford: Stanford University Press.

Buck-Morss, S. (2000). Hegel and Haiti. *Critical Inquiry*, 26(4), 821–865.

Buggeln, M. & Wildt, M. (2014). Arbeit im Nationalsozialismus (Einleitung). In M. Buggeln & M. Wildt, eds., *Arbeit im Nationalsozialismus*. München: De Gruyter Oldenbourg, ix–xxvii.

Burke, E. ([1783]1981). Speech on Fox's India Bill. In *The Writings and Speeches of Edmund Burke, vol. 5: India, Madras and Bengal 1774–1785*, ed. P. J. Marshall & P. Langford. Oxford: Clarendon Press, 380–451.

Caird, E. (1907). *Lay Sermons and Addresses Delivered in the Hall of Balliol College, Oxford*, Glasgow: Maclehose.

Clarkson, T. ([1786]2010). *An Essay on the Slavery and Commerce of the Human Species, Particularly the African*, in Clarkson & Cugoano, 57–219.

Cohn, B. (1989). Law and the Colonial State in India. In J. Starr & J. Collier, eds., *History and Power in the Study of Law: New Directions in Legal Anthropology*. Ithaca, NY: Cornell University Press, 131–152.

~~Coleman,~~ N.A.T. (manuscript). Hegel and Heyrick.

Conrad, S. (2012). *German Colonialism: A Short History*, trans. S. O'Hagan, Cambridge: Cambridge University Press.

Creuzer, G. F. (1810–1812). *Symbolik und Mythologie der alten Völker, besonders der Griechen*, 4 Vols., Leipzig: Leske.

Davis, A. (1971). *Lectures on Liberation*, [no place]. archive.org/details/ AngelaDavis-LecturesOnLiberation.

Davis, D. B. (1999). *The Problem of Slavery in the Age of Revolution, 1770–1823*, 2nd ed., New York: Oxford University Press.

de Azara, F. ([1809]1810). *Reise nach Süd-Amerika von Don Felix von Azara in den Jahren 1781 bis 1801*, trans. C. A. Walkenaer & P. C. Weyland, Berlin: Vossische Buchhandlung.

de Pauw, C. (1768). *Recherches philosophiques sur les Américains, ou Mémoires intéressants pour servir à l'Histoire de l'Espèce Humaine*, 2 Vols., Berlin: Decker.

Dumas, P. (2016). *Proslavery Britain: Fighting for Slavery in an Era of Abolition*, New York: Palgrave Macmillan.

Dumas, P. (2017). The Edinburgh Review, the Quarterly Review, and the Contributions of the Periodical to the Slavery Debates. *Slavery & Abolition*, 38(3), 559–576.

Dussel, E. (1995). *The Invention of the Americas: Eclipse of the 'Other' and the Myth of Modernity*, trans. M. Barber, New York: Continuum.

References

Egid, J. (2024). Hegel, Italian Orientalism and the Hatäta Zär'a Yaʿəqob: Africa in the Philosophy of History and the History of Philosophy. *Hegel Bulletin*, First view.

Elliott, J. H. (2006). *Empires of the Atlantic World: Britain and Spain in America, 1492–1830*, New Haven: Yale University Press.

Fanon, F. ([1952]2021). *Black Skin, White Masks*, trans. R. Philcox, London: Penguin.

Fenske, H. (1991). Ungeduldige Zuschauer: Die Deutschen und die europäische Expansion 1815–1880. In W. Reinhard, ed., *Imperialistische Kontinuität und nationale Ungeduld im 19. Jahrhundert*. Frankfurt a.M.: Fischer, 87–123.

Ferguson, A. ([1767]1996). *An Essay on the History of Civil Society*, Cambridge: Cambridge University Press.

Ferreiro, H. (2019). Hegel y América Latina: Entre el diagnóstico de la brecha de desarrollo y el eurocentrismo. *Hermenéutica Intercultural*, 31, 187–208.

FitzClarence, G. A. F. (1819). *Journal of a Route across India, through Egypt, to England, in the Latter End of the Year 1817, and the Beginning of 1818*, London: Thomas Davison. https://archive.org/details/journalofrouteac00munsrich/.

Forster, G. (1789). Vorrede des Übersetzers. In Keate, G. *Nachrichten von den Pelew-Inseln in der Westgegend des stillen Oceans* [...], trans. G. Forster. Hamburg: Hoffmann, xxix–xlviii.

Fragoso, J. (2015). E as plantations viraram fumaça: nobreza principal da terra, Antigo Regime e escravidão mercantil. *História*, 34(2), 58–107.

Freire, P. ([1970]2017). *Pedagogy of the Oppressed*, London: Penguin.

Fuchs, B. (2008). The Spanish Race. In Greer Mignolo, W. & Quilligan, M., eds., *Rereading the Black Legend: The Discourses of Religious and Racial Difference in the Renaissance Empires*, Chicago: University of Chicago Press, 88–98.

Ganson, B. A. (2003). *The Guaraní under Spanish Rule in the Río de La Plata*, Stanford: Stanford University Press.

Gerbi, A. ([1955]2000). *La disputa del Nuovo Mondo*, Milan: Adelphi.

Getachew, A. (2019). *Worldmaking after Empire: The Rise and Fall of Self-Determination*, Princeton: Princeton University Press.

Gilroy, P. (2011). *Darker than Blue: On the Moral Economies of Black Atlantic Culture*. Cambridge, MA: Harvard University Press.

Greer, M., Mignolo, W. & Quilligan, M., eds. (2008). *Rereading the Black Legend: The Discourses of Religious and Racial Difference in the Renaissance Empires*, Chicago: University of Chicago Press.

Guha, R. (2003). *History at the Limit of World-History*, New York: Columbia University Press.

Habib, M. A. R. (2017). *Hegel and Empire: From Postcolonialism to Globalism*, Cham: Palgrave Macmillan.

Harris, K. A. (manuscript). Black Hegelianism.

Harvey, D. (1981). The Spatial Fix – Hegel, von Thunen, and Marx. *Antipode*, 13(3), 1–12.

Hirschman, A. (1976). On Hegel, Imperialism, and Structural Stagnation. *Journal of Development Economics*, 3(1), 1–8.

Hoffheimer, M. (1993). Does Hegel Justify Slavery? *The Owl of Minerva*, 25(1), 118–119.

Hoffheimer, M. (2001). Hegel, Race, Genocide. *The Southern Journal of Philosophy*, 39(S1), 35–62.

Hogan, B. (2023). Reading Fanon on Hegel. *Philosophy Compass*, 18(8), 1–11.

Ilieva, E. (2024). The Afterlives of the Dialectic: C.L.R. James's Hegel. *Hegel Bulletin*, 45(1), 144–165.

Jaarte, M. (2024). Colonial Slavery, the Lord-Bondsman Dialectic, and the St. Louis Hegelians. *Hegel Bulletin*, 45(1), 43–64.

James, C. L. R. ([1938]1989). *The Black Jacobins: Toussaint L'Ouverture and the San Domingo Revolution*, London: W.H. Allen.

James, C. L. R. ([1948]1980). *Notes on Dialectics*: *Hegel, Marx, Lenin*. Westport: Lawrence Hill.

James, C. L. R. (2000). Lectures on the Black Jacobins. *Small Axe*, 8, 65–112.

James, D. (2020). Social Organisms: Hegel's Organisational View of Social Functions. In R. Hufendiek, D. James & R. van Riel, eds., *Social Functions in Philosophy*. London: Routledge, 219–246.

James, D. & Knappik, F. (2023). Exploring the Metaphysics of Hegel's Racism: The Teleology of the 'Concept' and the Taxonomy of Races. *Hegel Bulletin*, 44(1), 99–126.

James, D. & Knappik, F. (forthcoming). G.W.F. Hegel, Frantz Fanon, and Angela Davis on Recognition, Slavery, and Liberation. In M. Congdon & T. Khurana, eds., *The Philosophy of Recognition: Expanded Perspectives on a Fundamental Concept*. London: Routledge.

Kant, I. (1902ff.). *Gesammelte Schriften*, ed. Königlich-Preussische Akademie der Wissenschaften zu Berlin, Berlin: de Gruyter.

Kaymaz, N. (2019). From Imperialism to Internationalism: British Idealism and Human Rights. *The International History Review*, 41(6), 1235–1255.

Kuch, H. (2013). *Herr und Knecht: Anerkennung und symbolische Macht im Anschluss an Hegel*, Frankfurt: Campus.

Leuze, R. (1975). *Die außerchristlichen Religionen bei Hegel*, Göttingen: Vandenhoeck & Ruprecht.

Lewis, G. K. (2000). Proslavery Ideology. In V. Shepherd & H. Beckles, eds., *Caribbean Slavery in the Atlantic World*. Kingston: Ian Randal, 544–579.

Lindley, M. F. (1926). *The Acquisition and Government of Backward Territory in International Law*, London: Longmans, Green.

Maldonado-Torres, N. (2007). On the Coloniality of Being: Contributions to the Development of a Concept. *Cultural Studies*, 21(2), 240–270.

Mander, W. J. (2011). *British Idealism: A History*, Oxford: Oxford University Press.

Mascat, J. M. H. (2014). Hegel and the Black Atlantic: Universalism, Humanism and Relation. In N. Dhawan, ed., *Decolonizing Enlightenment: Transnational Justice, Human Rights and Democracy in a Postcolonial World*. Berlin: Budrich, 93–114.

Matthews, G. (2006). *Caribbean Slave Revolts and the British Abolitionist Movement*, Baton Rouge: Louisiana State University Press.

Mbembe, A. (2007). L'Afrique de Nicolas Sarkozy. *Mouvements*, 52(4), 65–73.

McCarney, J. (2012). *Routledge Philosophy Guidebook to Hegel on History*, London: Routledge.

Meek, R. (1976). *Social Science and the Ignoble Savage*, Cambridge: Cambridge University Press.

Megay, E. (1958). Treitschke Reconsidered: The Hegelian Tradition of German Liberalism. *Midwest Journal of Political Science*, 2(3), 298–317.

Meiners, C. (1790). Ueber die Natur der afrikanischen Neger (und die davon abhängige Befreyung, oder Einschränkung der Schwarzen). *Göttingisches historisches Magazin*, 6, 385–456.

Midgley, C. (1992). *Women against Slavery: The British Campaigns, 1780–1870*, London: Routledge.

Mill, J. (1817). *The History of British India*, 3 Vols., London: Baldwin. archive.org/details/in.ernet.dli.2015.103762/.

Millar, J. ([1779]2006). *The Origin of the Distinction of Ranks [. . .]*, Carmel: Liberty Fund.

Mills, C. (2013). An Illuminating Blackness. *The Black Scholar*, 43(4), 32–37.

Moltmann, G., ed. (1979). *Aufbruch nach Amerika: Friedrich List und die Auswanderung aus Baden und Württemberg 1816/17: Dokumentation einer sozialen Bewegung*, Tübingen: Wunderlich.

Montesquieu. ([1748]1995). *De l'Esprit des lois*, 2 Vols., Paris: Gallimard.

Morefield, J. (2014). *Empires without Imperialism: Anglo-American Decline and the Politics of Deflection*, New York: Oxford University Press.

Muirhead, J. H. ([1900]1997). What Imperialism Means. In D. Boucher, ed., *The British Idealists*. Cambridge: Cambridge University Press, 237–252.

Murthy, V. (2024). Rescuing Hegel from Eurocentrism: Oriental Reconstructions of Hegel's Orient. *Hegel Bulletin*. First view, 45(2): 368–395.

Muthu, S. (2003). *Enlightenment against Empire*, Princeton: Princeton University Press.

Narváez León, Á. (2019). *Hegel y la economía mundial: crítica y génesis de la economía política del colonialismo*, Valparaíso: Ediciones universitarias de Valparaíso.

Neuhouser, F. (2000). *Foundations of Hegel's Social Theory: Actualizing Freedom*. Cambridge, MA: Harvard University Press.

Oquendo, A. (1999). Freedom and Slavery in Hegel. *History of Philosophy Quarterly*, 16, 437–464.

Pagden, A. (1995). *Lords of All the World: Ideologies of Empire in Spain, Britain and France c.1500-c.1800*, New Haven: Yale University Press.

Paquette, G. (2012). Colonies and Empire in the Political Thought of Hegel and Marx. In S. Muthu, ed., *Empire and Modern Political Thought*. Cambridge: Cambridge University Press, 292–323.

Park, P. (2013). *Africa, Asia, and the History of Philosophy*, Albany: State University of New York Press.

Patterson, O. (1982). *Slavery and Social Death: A Comparative Study*, Cambridge, MA: Harvard University Press.

Pettit, P. (2015). *The Robust Demands of the Good: Ethics with Attachment, Virtue, and Respect*. Oxford: Oxford University Press.

Pinkard, T. (2017). *Does History Make Sense? Hegel on the Historical Shapes of Justice*, Cambridge, MA: Harvard University Press.

Pitts, J. (2005). *A Turn to Empire: The Rise of Imperial Liberalism in Britain and France*, Princeton: Princeton University Press.

Pradella, L. (2014). Hegel, Imperialism, and Universal History. *Science & Society*, 78(4), 426–453.

Rajan, B. (1999). *Under Western Eyes: India from Milton to Macaulay*, Durham: Duke University Press.

Rathore, A. S. & Mohapatra, R. (2018). *Hegel's India: A Reinterpretation, with Texts*, New Delhi: Oxford University Press.

Ray, R. K. (1998). Indian Society and the Establishment of British Supremacy, 1765–1818. In P. J. Marshall, ed., *The Oxford History of the British Empire. Vol. 2: The Eighteenth Century*. Oxford: Oxford University Press, 508–529.

Raynal, G.-T. (1770). *Histoire philosophique et politique des établissements et du commerce des Européens dans les deux Indes*, 6 Vols., Amsterdam: s.n.

Renault, M. (2016). Decolonizing Revolution with C.L.R. James: Or, What Is to Be Done with Eurocentrism? *Radical Philosophy*, 199, 35–45. www.radicalphilosophy.com/article/decolonizing-revolution-with-c-l-r-james.

Renault, M. (2021). Counter-Violence, a 'Hegelian' Myth: Minor Variations on the Master-Slave Dialectic. *Radical Philosophy*, 210, 21–32. www.radicalphilosophy.com/article/counter-violence-a-hegelian-myth.

Rosenkranz, K. (1844). *Georg Wilhelm Friedrichs Leben*, Berlin: Duncker & Humblot.

Said, E. ([1978]2019). *Orientalism*, London: Penguin.

Schneider, H. & Waszek, N., eds. (1997). *Hegel in der Schweiz (1793–1796)*, Frankfurt a.M.: Lang.

Serequeberhan, T. (1989). The Idea of Colonialism in Hegel's Philosophy of Right. *International Philosophical Quarterly*, 29(3), 301–318.

Sharma, A. (2017). *The Ruler's Gaze: A Study of British Rule over India from a Saidian Perspective*, Noida: HarperCollins.

Shaw, S. (2013). *W.E.B. Du Bois and the Souls of Black Folk*. Chapel Hill: University of North Carolina Press.

Smith, A. ([1776]1999). *The Wealth of Nations*, London: Penguin.

Smith, M. (2010). Introduction. In Clarkson, T. & Cugoano, O. eds., *Essays on the Slavery and Commerce of the Human Species*. Peterborough: Broadview Press, 9–47.

Steuart, J. (1767). *An Inquiry into the Principles of Political Economy [. . .]*, London: Millar & Cadell. archive.org/details/inquiryintoprinc01steu.

Stone, A. (2020). Hegel and Colonialism. *Hegel Bulletin*, 41(2), 247–270.

Tallmadge [jr., J.]. (1819). Rede des Herrn Tallmadge, aus Newyork, im Hause der Repräsentanten der Vereinigten Staaten über die Sclaverei der Neger. *Minerva*, 111, 161–202.

Tavarès, F. (1992). Hegel et Haiti ou le silence de Hegel sur Saint Domingue. *Chemins Critiques*, 2(3), 113–131.

Tibebu, T. (2011). *Hegel and the Third World: The Making of Eurocentrism in World History*, Syracuse: Syracuse University Press.

Turley, D. (1991). *The Culture of English Antislavery, 1780–1860*, London: Routledge.

Urquidez, A. (2020). *(Re-)Defining Racism: A Philosophical Analysis*, Cham: Palgrave Macmillan.

Varma, P. (2012). *Becoming Indian: The Unfinished Revolution of Culture and Identity*, London: Penguin.

Voltaire. ([1759]1969). *Candide ou l'optimisme*, Paris: Bordas.

Waszek, N. (1988). *The Scottish Enlightenment and Hegel's Account of 'Civil Society'*, Dordrecht: Kluwer.

Westphal, K. (2017). Hegel's Natural Law Constructivism: Progress in Principle and in Practice. In T. Brooks & S. Stein, eds., *Hegel's Political Philosophy: On the Normative Significance of Method and System*. Oxford: Oxford University Press, 253–279.

Williams, E. ([1944]2022). *Capitalism and Slavery*, London: Penguin.

Wood, A. (1990). *Hegel's Ethical Thought*, Cambridge: Cambridge University Press.

Zantop, S. (1997). *Colonial Fantasies: Conquest, Family, and Nation in Precolonial Germany, 1770–1870*, Durham: Duke University Press.

Acknowledgements

We are grateful to Alison Stone for written comments on the whole manuscript; to George Felix Cabral de Souza, Gwinyai Machona, Matthew Congdon, and Karen Ng for their feedback on Sections 2, 3, and 6, with Congdon and Ng specifically offering comments during a workshop they hosted at Vanderbilt University; to Nonhle Beryl, Ben Grindel, Thea Halbach, Jesko Hennig, Leonie Himmerich, Jeanne Kayatz, Nadja Lang, David Müller, Peter Niesen, Simon Pistor and Marie Wuth for their comments during a book symposium that Peter Niesen kindly organised at the University of Hamburg; and to audiences in Bergen, Berlin, Bielefeld, Bochum, Bremen, Dresden, Leipzig, Leuven, London, Nashville, New Orleans, Purdue and online. Extracts from PhR are quoted by permission from Cambridge University Press.

Cambridge Elements ≡

The Philosophy of Georg Wilhelm Friedrich Hegel

Sebastian Stein
Heidelberg University

Sebastian Stein is a Research Associate at Heidelberg University. He is co-editor of *Hegel's Political Philosophy* (2017), *Hegel and Contemporary Practical Philosophy* (with James Gledhill, 2019) and *Hegel's Encyclopedic System* (2021), and has authored several journal articles and chapters on Aristotle, Kant, post-Kantian idealism and (neo-)naturalism.

Joshua Wretzel
Pennsylvania State University

Joshua Wretzel is Assistant Teaching Professor of Philosophy at the Pennsylvania State University. He is the co-editor of *Hegel's Encyclopedic System* and *Hegel's Encyclopedia of the Philosophical Sciences: A Critical Guide* (Cambridge). His articles on Hegel and the German philosophical tradition have appeared in multiple edited collections and peer-reviewed journals, including the *European Journal of Philosophy* and *International Journal for Philosophical Studies*.

About the Series

These Elements provide insights into all aspects of Hegel's thought and its relationship to philosophical currents before, during, and after his time. They offer fresh perspectives on well-established topics in Hegel studies, and in some cases use Hegelian categories to define new research programs and to complement existing discussions.

Cambridge Elements ≡

The Philosophy of Georg Wilhelm Friedrich Hegel

Elements in the Series

Hegel and Heidegger on Time
Ioannis Trisokkas

Hegel and Colonialism
Daniel James and Franz Knappik

A full series listing is available at: www.cambridge.org/EPGH

Printed by Libri Plureos GmbH in Hamburg, Germany